Triggered

The Attack on Common Sense in
Modern America

J. P. Leask

Print ISBN: 979-8-9946300-2-0

Contents

To all Americans—
From every place, background, and walk of life who live
with hope in their hearts and trust in one another.

Who choose optimism over cynicism, and faith over fear.

Who see in one another not strangers, but neighbors
who reach across differences and try to understand one
another.

To the visionaries and doers, the builders and believers,
who have conviction that our shared story is not yet
finished.

To those who courageously strive to build something
better together.

And who search for common ground in our shared love
of country.

To all Americans who keep faith in a bright future
In pursuit of the purpose & promise of
the American Dream.

Declaration

This book is about Common Sense.
You and your beliefs, even if they're different than mine,
are safe from attack.

This book is about the divisiveness in our country.
It is not a political book.

It is a book that tells a story of current societal trends.

No political parties or current politicians are mentioned.

This book is designed to spark new thoughts rather than
trigger old emotions.

A Personal Note from the Author:

I want to start a conversation as a friend, with the goal of building a great society, a better America.

I want to discuss the division in our country by pointing out the underlying factors beneath the surface of politics, using language and a sense of the world that foster common ground rather than trigger animosity.

Common sense is not so common anymore. If we can understand its value and apply it to our lives, we will have learned a lot. Life is not meant to be complicated. It is only when we get away from common sense that we lose ourselves in confusion.

For 25 years, I have been teaching my children how to live a fulfilling and meaningful life through a simple three-part formula. I began writing a book to pass on that wisdom, only to discover that the insights are even more relevant and urgent today to more people than just my children. That's how this book was born.

This book is not a formula for life solutions or a

prescription for our current challenges. Rather, it is a connecting of dots to sort out issues and dangerous trends. I aim to present options going forward that challenge you to put all bias aside and reflect on American society and your role in it.

Our children, those who inherit this country, deserve for us to at least try to understand one another. Would you agree with that?

What you can get out of this book

To see the world objectively, free of preconceived notions and biases. Seeing things as they are, how they should be, and how everything is connected. To, as Jeff Bezos says, look deeper into issues with a 'beginner's mindset,' being open to new ideas.

To view things from a different perspective: how we got here, what is under the surface, and what is yet to come. To take a more rationally-centered rather than emotionally-scattered take on our world. To come away with a conversational structure that will allow you to discuss daily life and current events without feuding over politics.

Mostly, to have a framework for dialogue including the right kind of questions to help explore the current condition of the American Dream and what it still might become.

Echoes from our Founding Fathers

"Moderation in temper is always a virtue; but moderation in principle is always a vice."

— Thomas Paine

"The advancement and diffusion of knowledge is the only guardian of true liberty."

— James Madison

"Truth will ultimately prevail where there is pains to bring it to light."

— George Washington

"The best thing to give to your enemy is forgiveness; to an opponent, tolerance; to a friend, your heart; to your child, a good example; to a father, deference; to your mother, conduct that will make her proud of you; to yourself, respect; to all others, charity."

— Benjamin Franklin

"Eternal vigilance is the price of liberty."

— John Jay

"The boisterous sea of liberty is never without a wave."

— Thomas Jefferson

Introduction

The voices of our country's Founding Fathers have faded, yet the spirit behind their beliefs and fight for liberty endures. They held a compelling vision – to break free from tyranny and build an independent nation grounded in faith and courage. They united the common man behind a common cause: independence and liberty. A noble fight.

Unfortunately, that same fight continues. America is weathering through a sea of change. We all sense it. Our current battle is cloaked in covert forces stirring unrest across our sea of liberty. These interconnected forces linger like an insidious plague, distorting the fabric of modern America and weakening our ability to live as our Founding Fathers fought for.

Everything is connected. Yes, everything.

Only with vigilance and insight can we recognize and comprehend these intertwined forces and shape a new world rising upon a tide of resurgent spirit.

One of the great laments of our time is that we are being ripped apart by political polarization. But the real damage is being done by stealthy powers hiding underneath the cloak of politics. Until we face the truth, we will remain divided – fueling a tragic fate.

What's really going on?

This book is derived from the foundational wisdom of Thomas Paine's 1776 pamphlet, *Common Sense:*

- *The present state of America is truly alarming to every man who is capable of reflection.*
- *A long habit of not thinking a thing wrong gives it a superficial appearance of being right.*
- *Time makes more converts than reason*

Two and a half centuries later, America's state is again alarming. Common sense has given way to twisted values and destructive attitudes. We're becoming a nation at war with itself – caught between the past and the future, between tradition and misguided progress. It's time for a reality check.

Sinister forces disfigure our way of life.

Their impact is subtle yet substantial, quietly extinguishing the flames of passion, purpose, and community. Our society bears the mark of decline. There's a storm brewing, and it's raising the waves of the once tranquil sea of liberty.

Take a moment to step back from your busy life and reflect on what is happening in America. If you do, you'll see the signs: we've traded real connection for virtual validation, curiosity for convenience, and courage for comfort. The patterns are clearly disturbing.

Warning Signs of Our Societal Decline:

We used to take pictures of nature or family on our vacations.
Then, we didn't care much to take many photos.
Now, we take photos all the time... but mostly of ourselves (selfies).

We used to be self-sufficient.
Then, we leaned on others to help.
Now, we have an app or AI for everything.

We used to go outside and explore with other kids routinely.
Then, we kids got into supervised activities
Now, kids stay inside on phones/computers.

We used to, as witnesses to a street crime, assist the victim.
Then, we stood idly by without getting involved.
Now, we record the episode on cell phones & post it to social media.

Introduction

It used to be that women appreciated men holding a door open.
Then, women insisted they could open the door themselves.
Now, men worry they can get sued for harassment for being polite.

We used to do show-and-tell in grade school.
Then, we performed in scripted plays.
Now, teachers show & tell things children shouldn't be exposed to.

We used to welcome new neighbors with baked goods.
Then, we, at most, said 'Hi' to them when we saw them walk the dog.
Now, we complain about all our neighbors on Nextdoor.com.

We used to go to the library or bookstore to enable learning.
Then, we just went online to Amazon to buy books.
Now, we don't read books; we use Facebook to impart wisdom.

We used to sit on our porch, waving at our neighbors doing the same.
Then, on a summer night, we would throw a block party to socialize.
Now, using social media we gather for mischief as a flash mob.

We used to leave our doors unlocked as we welcomed visitors.

Then, we locked our doors, only opening them to familiar faces.

Now, with security systems, we run for cover when someone knocks.

A new social order is forming, reshaping how we think, live, and relate.

As Ferris Bueller once said, "Life moves pretty fast. If you don't stop and look around once in a while, you could miss it."

In the pages ahead, you'll see a clear-eyed view of the cultural and social forces threatening to unravel our nation's fabric. This blessed nation can still provide a great future for everyone; however, to achieve that end, we must be vigilant and prepared to protect our way of life.

To establish a foundation for our journey we will get grounded in three spirit-infused principles – truths once held by our Founding Fathers.

.

Part 1
Getting Grounded

Chapter 1

Foundational Principles

By nature, we yearn for a better future, a life of success, fulfillment, and meaning.

We seek significance not merely in the form of achievement, but by congruence between who we are, where we fit, and what we hold to be true. In society, this quest can be understood through three deeply connected dimensions, which we will explore here. Together, they form a psychological and spiritual frame for identity, motivation, and sense of purpose.

Becoming

Our country was founded on simple truths, core beliefs, and common sense. Key among these ideals are freedom and opportunity. The freedom to choose and the opportunity to have. To choose what we want is an elemental human desire that our country's Founding Fathers, in the Declaration of Independence, framed foundationally as unalienable rights: life, liberty, and the pursuit of happiness. Although it is natural to feel entitled to these rights and particularly to feel deserving of happiness, it is the enlightened minority among us who realize that to have, we must do.

To Do, we must Become.

Having is not possible without the doing, and the doing is not possible without the becoming. Indeed, the having is a function of doing and becoming. To achieve financial success, for example, a professional must provide value to their employer or to the marketplace as an entrepreneur. Yet, to do the work well, the professional must become a highly capable team player or business leader. And of course, your skills and competence always limit your ability to do or, if you are so inclined, your sneaky and shrewd prowess of cheating the system without being caught, all developed by virtue of who you have become.

It all starts and ends with Identity, the person, the community, and the country we've become. Our natural selves, emerging from our heritage, lineage, parentage, tutelage, and village, are what we build upon as we evolve as individuals. The problem is that many people struggle to become who they want to be because they remain too attached to who they have been. Or, they're not sure who they want to be, as opined by Lily Tomlin, "I always wanted to be somebody, but now I realize I should have been more specific!"

Becoming is a continual process, a continuous evolution with ebbs and flows, peaks and valleys, phases and seasons, and backtracks and breakthroughs. Becoming is a harmony of purposeful progression on one hand and serendipitous enjoyment on the other. The art of becoming is fluid, like dancing, rather than rigid, like marching. When it's all said and done, becoming is what life is all about.

The cup of having never fills, whereas becoming continuously fills you with your true self, the music you dance to. It offers the ultimate measure of success. You won't find true peace through having, only through becoming the person you always wanted to be. Becoming serves as both a tollgate and a destination on the road to Success.

We are hard-wired to desire growth in our relationships, careers, and contributions to others, ultimately striving to become as close to our ideal selves as possible. The desire for personal growth is deeply ingrained in our psyche. You can have countless friends, a high-salaried job, a successful business, a loving family life, and all the trappings of success, but if you are not experiencing growth in at least one aspect of your life, you will inevitably feel a void.

People often conflate what society, parents, and their culture want them to want, versus what they genuinely desire. When your yearning doesn't match up with culturally accepted aspirations, resisting social pressure to conform becomes difficult. But it pays dividends: a common regret is having lived the life others wanted for us rather than the one we wanted for ourselves.

Our identity is tied to the things we want. For example, and be honest here: Did you purchase that luxury car because you wanted a luxury car or because you wanted to become a luxury car owner? You think you own that car. But in reality, the car also owns you - at least one key part of your identity.

Yes, our sense of identity rules our actions. And be wary, be purposeful in your actions, as each choice, every action you take, is a vote for the person you are becoming.

Experience and conscience teach us that authenticity to our inner self beats wearing a mask to fit in – even if it means dancing to the beat of your own drum.

Belonging

We aren't designed to live as a one-man band, though. We are social creatures. Baumeister and Leary's seminal paper on belongingness posits that "Much of what human beings do is done in the service of belonging-ness." They argue that many social compulsions – needs for power, intimacy, approval, achievement, and affiliation – all stem from the need to belong.

Abraham Maslow, the American psychologist who in the 1940's devised the famous Maslow's hierarchy of needs, a theory of psychological health, also suggested that the need to belong is a major source of human motivation. In fact, in his hierarchy of needs he placed belonging right after physiological and safety & security needs in terms of fundamental importance.

Relationship needs run so deep that we relentlessly strive for belonging and meaningful connections within our faith, family, and friend networks. We crave fulfilling social interactions, fellowship, empathy, and love. After all, the dance of life is enjoyable only in social interplay with others.

Belonging is when you want to be with others who want you there, while fitting in is when you want to be with others who don't care if you're there or not. Belonging is a bidirectional state of mind. Opportunity abounds when you surround yourself with folks who fight for you to belong in rooms you aren't already in.

While pursuing opportunity and growth as captains of our own destiny, the journey isn't all about us. It is also about others within our sphere who can benefit from our efforts. First Lady Eleanor Roosevelt said, "For what keeps our interest in life and makes us look forward to tomorrow is giving pleasure to other people." Live purposefully pursuing your best self while giving unselfishly to others, and happiness will find you deep within your soul, separate from external validation.

Self-help guru Wayne Dyer says, "What other people think of me is none of my business." That's good advice regarding personal impressions, particularly from people who don't know you. Max Ehrmann's *Desiderata* adds: "If you compare yourself to others, you may become vain or bitter, for always there will be greater and lesser persons than yourself." True belonging is not about comparing, judging, or seeking acceptance – it's seeing and connecting to the common human spirit in others.

Humans are not much different from the rest of creation in that we, and other things in nature, don't live for ourselves. Trees don't eat the fruit they bear, the sun does not shine for itself, a flower's fragrance is not for the flower, bees don't dance for themselves, nor do birds sing solely for selfish purposes.

There is a harmony, a symbiosis in nature and in the best aspects of human nature, that benefits individuals mutually. Living for each other, in a sense belonging to each other, is the rule of nature. Indeed, one can say that the meaning of life is to find your gift and the purpose of life is to give it away!

To be an effective giver, you must reset the balance between your wants and needs with the needs, wants, and liberties of others. But the payoff of a giving mind-set, of becoming a generous giver, is a life of fulfilment and the power of becoming your best self. The standard to strive for is not a standard of living but rather a standard of giving.

It is often the case that at life's end, our most fond memories and those we take with us in death are of the relationships we cherished the most. Not the things or material possessions, of course, but the relationships. In that way, belonging is both a toll gate and an ultimate destination on the road to Fulfillment.

Believing

We can only become who we aspire to be through growth and lessons learned. We grow in knowledge, skill, competence, and our ability to effect desired outcomes.

Your daily life follows lessons learned and the associated rules of thought and behavior that are programmed into your conscious and subconscious mind. This programming, a key belief influencer, largely comes from life experience, social interaction, and the stories we hear from others.

To experience, learn, and grow fully toward our desired becoming, we must guard against the programming of our minds. Proverbs 4:23 prescribes: "More than anything you guard, protect your mind, for life flows from it."

Guard your mind by filling it first with the right thinking. Socrates said, "The unexamined life is not worth living", advocating for discernment – a wise way of judging between things. Discerning wisdom is one of the most effective tools for maintaining an agile mind, finding meaning, and enabling personal growth.

With wisdom we can apply knowledge, experience, good judgment, and common sense to make sound decisions and act productively. Our search for wisdom and truth is a complex endeavor. We acquire knowledge through experience and by learning from various sources. However, not only are many information sources prejudiced and their content distorted, but we, as the receivers, are also culpable for accepting untruths due to certain cognitive biases. These biases can have us unknowingly twist the truth as we process information.

The following five most common cognitive biases create mayhem in our attempts to acquire knowledge:

1. *Dunning-Kruger Effect:* People with limited competence in a particular domain overestimate their abilities.
2. *Confirmation bias:* We tend to remember and

give credence to information that confirms our perceptions.

3. *Availability Cascade:* Collective beliefs gain more traction with public repetition.
4. *Framing effect:* We often draw different conclusions depending on how the information is presented.
5. *Law of Triviality:* We give disproportionate weight to simple, trivial issues while ignoring more important, complex issues.

Despite incredible advances in scientific, technological, and human social knowledge, we still know very little about the entirety of our world. Neil DeGrasse Tyson, popular American astrophysicist, author, and science communicator, says, "We look out into the universe, and we look at all the forces that are driving what is going on, we actually can quantify how much of that we know, and it's about 4%." Significant gaps exist in our understanding of the world, the universe, and the human species. If you need more proof, scientists today <u>believe</u> we will <u>never</u> know all there is to know about the universe.

Where science leaves off, belief picks up. Belief leans on trust, faith, and confidence to bridge fact-based knowledge and individual reality. Unfortunately, our beliefs, no matter how well-founded, invariably fall short in unravelling ultimate truth.

Two schools of thought address ultimate truth. Some believe in universal truths – fundamental truths inherent in nature and human instincts. Absolute truthers subscribe to fundamental truth grounded in certain realities and standards, believing that objective reality exists. They think that the lack of absolute truths in science, morals, and ethics leads to confusion and chaos.

An opposing view, postmodernism, espouses that truth is relative, subjective and socially constructed. Relative truthers believe that right and wrong are relative, varying according to cultural context, time, place, and situation. They believe reality is merely perception and perspective, which is ultimately up to you to define. Relative truthers support an openness and 'do you' approach that often leads to a 'do it if it feels good' mentality.

We live in a chaotic world that requires soul-searching contemplation, awareness, and discernment to seek truth and the authentic self. We would be wise to heed the words of Robert Fulghum in his book *All I Really Need to Know I Learned in Kindergarten* where he says, "And then remember the Dick-and-Jane books and the first word you learned - the biggest word of all - LOOK."

The right mindset, placing faith in the future rather than clinging to hope, gives meaning to all we are and do, as we purposefully pursue becoming our best selves. We reveal our best selves when we believe in something bigger than ourselves. Believing serves as both a tollgate and a destination on the road to meaning.

We can't fully become through our life pursuits unless we Belong. We can't best align and elevate that pursuit to our chosen purpose unless we Believe. Finally, when we succeed in Becoming, we reinforce the cycle by deepening our Belonging and energizing our Belief.

Common Sense

The dimensions of Becoming, Belonging, and Believing are all interconnected in compelling ways. Brene Brown puts it this way, "True belonging is the spiritual practice of believing in and belonging to yourself so deeply that you can share your most authentic self with the world and find sacredness in both being a part of something and standing alone in the wilderness."

Looking back to the early American wilderness, we see how our forefathers established tight connections between these three dimensions. Our country's founders and early colonists were deeply committed to carving out a frontier life, establishing a community, and creating a successful experiment in democracy.

To survive in harsh conditions and fight against tyranny, the colonists mustered a profound sense of individual responsibility, belonging, and shared identity. To fight the good fight to establish a new nation. To endure and persevere, they leaned on faith and empowering beliefs. In taking on the challenge Becoming was their journey, Belonging was their home. Believing was their compass.

Thomas Paine's *Common Sense* pamphlet kickstarted the journey, producing groundswell support for freedom from English rule and taxation. Early America's freedom fighters became dedicated colony builders and patriots in pursuit of a liberating cause. Times were tough, yet with a shared vision and dream at their back, colonists persevered and prospered. Certain beliefs and values instilled and propagated across the new nation formed the core of their success.

These values took hold through common-sense principles under the banner of independence and liberty, framed in the art of becoming, the passion of belonging, and the inspiration of believing – all integral to the American Dream.

Common-Sense Values of Colonial Americans

BECOMING: Personal Virtues

Core Value	Description	Practical Effect
Self-Reliance	Provide for themselves & family.	Fostered initiative & accountability.
Courage	Facing hardship & risk was normal.	Cultivated toughness & resilience.
Integrity & Honor	Integrity thru Action not words.	Built trust in trade and governance.
Humility & Gratitude	Success was grace not entitlement.	Encouraged modesty & thankfulness.

BELONGING: Social and Civic Values

Core Value	Description	Practical Effect
Community	Depended on each other.	Created mutual trust & social bonds.
Common Purpose	People were connected & united.	Encouraged service, sacrifice & unity.
Duty & Responsibility	Obligation came before rights.	Infused resolve & accountability.
Respect Law & Order	Laws as compacts, not restrictions.	Built legitimacy & stability in society.

BELIEVING: Moral and Ethical Values

Core Value	Description	Practical Effect
Moral Principles	Faith in God; optimism.	Promoted honesty & fellowship.
Altruism & Charity	Helping others was a civic duty.	Built empathy & supportive culture.
Temperance & Thrift	Self-restraint- a guiding concept.	Enabled long term prosperity.
Work Ethic	Diligence was moral; laziness a sin.	Fueled self-discipline & growth.

In the following chapters, we will examine the current state and trends in our country to answer: Is the American Dream alive and well, or do attacks on its common-sense principles threaten prosperity in Modern America?

Part 2
Machinations and Trends

Chapter 2

Assault on Normalcy

Perhaps you have noticed the trends that are shaping our world in the 21st century. Perhaps you have recognized how those trends have taken our society backward. You might recognize the irony that these trends have been mainly ushered in by the kind of technology that has always promised a better life for us all. Although the tech-enabled better life hasn't fully materialized, it makes sense to reflect on the blessings ushered in by the technology that we now all take for granted.

Since the turn of the century, the rise of the internet, cell phones, and the resulting instantaneous interconnectivity have brought about significant improvements in many areas. Technology gives us fingertip access to a treasure trove of information. Technology enables us to automate much of what we previously had to handle manually or mentally. And technological developments in health, transportation, energy, and virtually every corner of society and commerce make things merely dreamed of yesterday possible today.

Technology does make our lives easier. Cell phones give us with more computing power in our hands than what was available to astronauts during their missions to the moon. Cell phones enable us to access information, communicate, and connect with others, regardless of our location. Our cell phone is simply an extension of ourselves, like another brain in our hand.

Technology has also given us the internet and social platforms with their virtual connecting prowess, allowing us to communicate with countless friends, influencers, or members of our own social group, as we might define it. With the internet and the various digital social platforms, we can share intimate details of our lives with countless folks all around the world. We can have many more friends or followers than ever before.

Here's the not-so-good news: those nifty perks are wrapped into a dispiriting package of devilish consequences. Our new age technology, along with social norms that have changed with it, have not only reshaped how we live but also are refashioning the beliefs and behaviors at the core of who we are and who we are becoming. And the story is not all sunshine and roses.

The technological advances that have overtaken us have been so quick and dramatic that we all see, feel, and experience the ramifications. Other trends have accompanied the tech revolution, those of mindset and behaviors that are also having a significant impact on our way of life. Technology progressing at a dizzying speed can indeed disrupt the pattern of our lives. But the change upon us has deeper roots than that. Our lives are changing because we are adapting to the modern world.

Our new age technology along with social norms that have changed with it, have not only reshaped how we live but also are refashioning the beliefs and behaviors at the core of who we are and who we are becoming.

Questions to Ponder:

1. What matters most in your search for meaning and fulfillment?
2. What are the defining societal trends of the 21st century born of our own decisions that negatively impact our ability to live well?

As you consider those questions, think about the various facets of living well and the mindsets, thoughts, behaviors, habits, and beliefs that contribute to it. Typical aspirations for living a well-lived life include fulfillment, purpose, love, progress, beauty, truth, justice, healthy relationships, and the ability to make a positive difference. Consider that although we speak of the desire to be happy, what we often really want is to be inspired to take action in becoming our best selves, progressing toward meaning and purpose, with loving relationships fueling our spirit along the way.

Let's take a practical and sensible look at recent history to recognize a few key trends that are shaping who we are and who and what we are becoming.

Social change in the 2000s is riding a wave of influence on a perfect storm of trends that have been brewing for a few decades and now continue to churn into a challenging legacy that is being left to our younger generations. Arguably, the most critical of the contributors to this legacy are:

1. An increasing reliance on comfort and a cushy existence
2. Disowning of the traditional family concept
3. Infatuation and pre-occupation with online social platforms

If you sense that America is facing nothing more than the usual trials of a fast-paced and changing world, what you read next may very well reframe your thinking. Our conversation will start, not with conclusions, but with first principles.

Chapter 3
Advantaged Lifestyle

Today's youth enjoy an advantaged lifestyle due to unprecedented prosperity in generational terms, enabled by technology, which makes many of life's challenges easier to manage. Older generations remember when we would have to spread and unfold an unwieldy map in the car to figure out how to get where we were going; we would hail a cab and wait and wait for our ride to come along; we would go to the video store to rent a movie on DVD to watch at home; we would actually go on blind dates; we would go to a book store to buy a book; we would write our own college essays.

Of course, with the internet, ChatGPT, and the rest of today's technology, all these things are either much easier to do or are, for the most part, done for us. Technology has indeed spoiled us in many ways. But alas, this cushy existence is making us soft.

To view our advantaged lifestyle from a broader historical perspective, consider what life was like for our grandparents' grandparents. Our earlier generation living in the mid-1800s had to toil torturously to prepare a home-cooked meal or to keep the homestead clean. One hundred and fifty years ago, meal preparation and household cleaning were tedious chores requiring quite grueling physical labor.

Prior to the twentieth century, cooking was normally performed on a coal or wood-burning stove. Preparing even a simple meal was time-consuming drudgery. Cast-iron stoves were exceptionally difficult to use. To prepare the stove, ashes from an old fire had to be removed, then paper and kindling had to be set inside. The dampers had to be carefully adjusted, and then a fire could be lit. The fire's intensity had to be continuously monitored as there were no thermostats to regulate the stove's temperature. Any time the fire weakened, fuel had to be added or the damper adjusted.

The cooking ritual in the 1800s required a stove to be continually replenished with new supplies of coal or wood, averaging fifty pounds a day. Altogether, from three to four hours every day were spent sifting ashes, adjusting dampers, lighting fires, and carrying coal or wood, and, of course, for our great-great-grandparents, preparing food called for more than just managing the cast-iron stove. Prior to 1900, there were few factory-prepared foods. Shopping was more like collective foraging, where every day folks played an integral role in the processing of raw food.

If you wanted chicken for dinner, you would buy poultry that was still alive, kill it, and then pluck it. Likewise, fish had to have scales removed. Green coffee had to be roasted and ground. Loaves of sugar had to be pounded, flour sifted, nuts shelled, and milk cream had to be churned to make butter. In many cases, fruits and vegetables were grown by the cook who now fulfilled the role of butcher, gardener, farmer, chef, and chief bottle washer.

Cleaning back then was just as arduous as cooking. The soot and smoke from coal and wood-burning stoves blackened walls and dirtied carpets and curtains. Gas and kerosene lamps left smelly deposits of black soot on furniture, ceilings and walls. On a regular basis, floors had to be scrubbed, rugs beaten, and windows washed.

Housework in nineteenth-century America was indeed back-breaking work. Before 1880, American households lacked many of the modern conveniences and labor-saving appliances we have today. There were no vacuum cleaners, toasters, processed and canned foods, gas stoves, automatic washing machines, or refrigerators. There was no hot and cold running water, for a hot shower, something we take for granted today. There were no automobiles, pick-up trucks, or SUVs... think about the inconvenience!

Then there were huge amounts of manure that piled up from horse-drawn carriages. A horse will, on average, produce between 15 and 35 pounds of manure per day. Consequently, the streets of our 19th-century cities were covered in horse manure, often to a depth of a foot or more. In the 1890s, New York City collected 500 tons of horse manure daily from more than 60,000 horses. The stacked manure attracted a huge number of flies, and when dried and ground up, it was blown everywhere.

So, when you think life in your modern world compared to yesteryear is a pile of sh*t, maybe you should recalibrate and think again, sunshine.

Yes, life in America has changed significantly with the assimilation of numerous incredible labor-saving technological advances. Although technology helps us save time, communicate more effectively and be more productive in all that we do, it makes us more dependent and spoiled. With all our modern technology, we are empowered and emancipated from the daily grind of yesteryear. Unfortunately, this emancipation has been combined with cultural forces to protect and pamper the growing ranks of the vulnerable who claim entitlement to a cushy existence.

The entitlement spawned Convenience Culture and later its cousin, Conspicuous Consumption, where privilege is professed and instant gratification is grabbed. In the post-World War II era, Americans have enjoyed a period of unprecedented prosperity. It started with things like fast food. Now, key services come to us quickly and on demand, such as ride-hailing, video streaming, online merchandise purchasing, and many more benefits of instant access to our needs and wants.

There has been human suffering since the dawn of man, but just think what your life would be like without automatic dishwashers, food delivery services, and car washes, cars that drive themselves, computers, the internet, and TV remotes. Think about how you'd respond when any of the aforementioned conveniences are not available or working properly. Your suffering would probably sound like #$@&%*!

Actor and comedian, Will Ferrell, said it this way: "Before you marry a person, you should first make them use a computer with slow internet to see who they really are!" We are like pampered kids, spoiled by our cushy existence and our dependence upon the tools and technology that run our lives. Clearly, the demand for and reliance on stress-free gratification, immediate indulgence, and comfort seem deeply entrenched in modern American life. Before we pamper ourselves, it would be commonsensical and constructive to recognize and activate this definition of maturity - the ability to widen the gap between impulse and action.

As we will explore further, when it comes to using our modern tech tools, it's not only our kids but our adults as well, who unfortunately, often overindulge, looking like a toddler clinging to a favorite, must-have toy.

Although technology helps us save time, communicate more effectively and be more productive in all that we do, it makes us more dependent and spoiled.

Technology is not a singular culprit, making us spoiled and soft. No, our spoiling has a few other root causes, including a few that hit close to home. Not only close to home but at home.

A reasonable argument can be made that what happens in America, in terms of trends, behaviors, and social mores, all gain traction within the home, within the family unit. Over the past couple of decades, our younger generations have had their Convenience Culture further greenlighted by a sidestepping of the school of hard knocks in large part enabled by overprotective parenting.

In an interview with Tom Bilyeu featured on YouTube, Simon Sinek comments on parenting in the 1990s and early 2000s by saying, "The generation that we call the millennials, too many who grew up subject to, not my words, failed parenting strategies. Where for example, they were told that they can have anything they want in life just because they want it."

In that interview, Sinek goes on to say that millennials often received special consideration in school or sports because their parents fought hard to secure it, including being given certain grades in school or trophies in sports that they didn't deserve, other than for simply being there and participating. Unfortunately, the participation medals and ribbons were counterproductive, as the benefactors —the kids —knew they hadn't earned them and were embarrassed that they had been undeservedly rewarded.

The lives of millennials were made easier because their parents adopted a newer form of parenting called helicopter parenting. "Helicopter parents" hovered overhead in a continuous holding pattern, overseeing and directing every part of their children's lives. These overprotective, overcontrolling micro-managers of their children's lives constantly work to remove social and emotional barriers to their kids' success. Kids of helicopter parents are coddled and enabled in and outside of the home and as a result are often disabled in their quest to grow up.

At home, most kids grow up hearing one of the most familiar words their parents say. That word is 'No!'... as in 'No, don't do that', 'No, you can't have that', 'No, you will have to wait'... The No programming has kids entering their teen years losing some of their wide-eyed wonder and eagerness for taking risks, innovating, and embracing new experiences.

By adolescence, the zeal and enabling 'little engine that could' mindset that flourishes in a kid's free-wheeling experiment of a world gives way to a structured and creativity-starving mantra of NO. Over-parenting, in general, has undoubtedly had a negative impact on the self-image, creativity, and coping skills of our children to the extent of limiting the future potential of many.

Our kids get exposed to more of the world at an early age by virtue of the Internet but despite that they tend to grow up slower. The stunting of maturity stems from trading real-world learning and personal growth for mindless hours spent virtually, caught in the dopamine-triggering trance of video games or social media.

Extemporaneous fun, whether making paper airplanes, building a fort out of cardboard boxes, or engaging in any form of improvisational play, has been replaced with hours spent pushing, twisting, and joy-sticking with video game controllers. As they grow a little older, they get hooked on cell phones.

It has gotten to the point where some thought leaders today are calling for blocking access to online social platforms to kids under adult age, as is done for other addictive vices like smoking and drinking. With no such restrictions in place now, many parents are challenged to resist their young children's demands for their own personal cell phones or internet access.

And so it goes with all sorts of privileges that our kids feel are their right to have, and which are there for the taking from their outmatched, doting, enabling, 'be you' philosophy-endorsing parents.

Troubling Signs of Being Spoiled; Have you seen folks...?

1. Displaying a Gimme Attitude
2. Demanding things Now or ASAP
3. Giving up Too Easily
4. Habitually thinking about Themselves
5. Having an incessant Sense of Entitlement
6. Complaining about Insignificant Issues
7. Never being Satisfied with what they Have
8. Complaining More Than Appreciating
9. Struggling with even Minor Disappointments
10. Being Co-Dependent

The soft and acquiescing parenting style that is common today has grownups pampering their children rather than preparing them. This is a real and significant problem, as arguably the number one job of a parent is to raise children to become responsible, self-sufficient, and contributing adult members of society who make the best of the opportunity to live out their life dreams and goals. Regrettably, the cushy lifestyle that our young generation enjoys has them unprepared to fend for themselves in the real world.

Is it any surprise that for the first time in over one hundred years, more young adults are living with their parents in their childhood home rather than on their own? In 1960, just 20% of young adults still lived at home with their parents. In 2018, that number jumped to just over 32%, a higher percentage than those living with a partner, spouse, or roommates!

In this country, there has long been an ideal called the American Dream. The *Oxford English Dictionary* defines the American dream as "the ideal that every citizen of the United States should have an equal opportunity to achieve success and prosperity through hard work, determination, and initiative." Today, it seems we enjoy a glimpse of that dream in our cushy, advantaged, and affluent lifestyle, yet often lack sustainable prosperity, as the hard work and determination part of the equation is often missing.

Compare the helicopter parenting of the 21st century with the parenting style typical of the 1960s and 1970s. Fifty years ago, there was a phenomenon called 'free range kids'. Free-range kids were given the freedom to go outside and play, invent games, experiment, and have fun with their friends any way they wanted just as long as they were home for dinner and didn't get into too much trouble. In that day, there was an abundance of spats between kids, countless bruises, cuts, and scrapes, and, at the same time, a lot of learning about nature, socializing with others, and learning the ways of the real world. Those were an integral part of growing up.

Here is a question to think about: "When was the last time you saw a kid in a cast?"

You might say that you have seen the tell-tale sign of broken bones recently, but then probably not. Our kids of yesteryear regularly suffered scrapes, got cut badly enough to require stitches, and quite often busted up their bodies enough to require a cast. The cast was a rite of passage, a sign that the adventurous, risk-taker had ventured out of his comfort zone and dared to try something he or she had never done. As homage and a show of support, it was common practice for friends, fellow fun junkies, to sign their name to the cast as a token of brotherhood. In effect, it acted as an endorsement of the risk-taking behavior.

Kids on the fun team relished the excitement that came with taking a chance by testing their skill and courage against a new and scary challenge; a challenge which was quite often prompted by a game of chicken or a friend's dare. It's crazy to suggest, as it might be taken out of context, but it might be better if we saw more kids in casts.

The unstructured and unsupervised play of yesteryear, a crucible of character that fostered creativity and helped develop social skills leading to self-sufficiency, is absent from the typical childhood of today. Kids need to be kids; they need to explore, experiment, take calculated risks, and play out their thirst for exhilaration and thrill. They need to take on the scary roller coaster, climb the towering oak tree, and rollerblade down the steep hill to become a brave apprentice in a world of challenging and often scary things.

The excessive coddling and overly curated lives of our youngsters make them soft, fragile, and bored, only to have them, in adolescence, rely on their cell phones, video games, or social platforms for solace.

Our participation trophy-toting younger generation has been incessantly pampered, lavished with praise, consoled, and pacified. This specialness, for which they are anointed, makes our younger generation self-centered and, arguably, more narcissistic.

The unstructured and unsupervised play of yesteryear, a crucible of character that fostered creativity and helped develop social skills leading to self-sufficiency, is absent from the typical childhood of today.

Jean Twenge, an American psychologist and professor of psychology at San Diego State, researching generational differences, has delved deeply into the question "Are we becoming more narcissistic?" In 2008, Twenge and her team compared 85 sets of completed Narcissistic Personality Inventory (NPI) assessments given to a random sampling of college-age participants between the years 1979 and 2006. In the final analysis, they found that narcissism levels among

US college students over that quarter of a century rose by 30 per cent.

This trend is disturbing as traits associated with narcissism (narcissistic personality disorder) include a grandiose sense of self-importance, frequent fantasies of having or deserving, and a need for admiration. What makes this upward trend of self-centeredness even more concerning is that it is far from abating and, indeed, is being further fueled by the interplay on popular social platforms. The platforms essentially normalize narcissism by welcoming the public parade of self-promotion, entitlement, and self-centeredness. Insidiously enough, this phenomenon is a self-perpetuating, ever-increasing cycle of indoctrination and reinforcement.

We are all self-centered to a degree, as we must be to control our lives. It is chronic narcissism referenced here, where one is perpetually afflicted with extreme egocentricity. This affliction is often associated with characteristics like aggression, manipulation, and behaviors that include harboring the conviction of entitlement, being dismissive of the needs of others, and lacking a sense of empathy or remorse. Chronic narcissism is essentially an obsession with self.

What makes chronic narcissism so debilitating to society is that it can be contagious. In a dog-eat-dog, I win, you lose world, my narcissism might very well provoke your further self-centeredness for you to get or regain your fair share of attention.

By creating a social playground where likes & followers are a measure of popularity and social credibility, the digital world fuels an obsession with lording over an upward spiraling level of histrionics and validation. Attention seeking works through a vicious cycle that has you reclaiming and further exacerbating your inborn egocentric persona, which in turn fans the flames of self-centeredness in others.

We will forever battle the compulsion for self-centeredness but there is a solution that we know how to use that can change the game.

Questions to Ponder:

1. In an increasingly risky and complicated world how should parents best help their children to succeed while also allowing the school of hard knocks to do much of the teaching?
2. As we mature in a life where, for the most part, our basic needs are met, what things should then become the unselfish desires of our hearts?

Chapter 4
Win-Win

Despite many of us succumbing to the temptation to be sinfully self-absorbed, we are, by design, social animals. We start as self-centered newborns, but that short-lived temperament eventually surrenders to our intrinsic need for interdependent relationships. Our instinctive drive to survive and ultimately to self-perpetuate as a species requires that we nurture ever more reliant and mutually beneficial relationships with others. Children growing up from early adolescence to adulthood progress in this way, and so too has our species, as a whole, over the course of history.

The story of our species' socialization begins with our prehistoric ancestors, who were preoccupied with safety, security, food and shelter. As humans acquired knowledge of agriculture and animal husbandry, we evolved from highly scattered, small bands of hunter-gatherers to co-located and communal farmers and ranchers.

Agriculture enabled early humans to form groups

with a shared goal of subsisting on the land's resources. From going solo or forming small bands as hunters, we began to gather in larger social groups to belong to a village or community. In these villages, we were able to provide sustenance, to experience and learn together, as well as pass our knowledge on to the next generation. Much later, the Industrial Age ushered in urbanization, with roads and infrastructure supporting trade with factory work becoming a common vocation.

Now, with the information age upon us, many people live wherever they want, as long as they have access to a phone, computer, and internet, which is sufficient for learning a skill and earning a living. Indeed, throughout history, our functional world has evolved from a band or tribe into a village into a metro-urbanized city or suburb, and now into a technologically connected planet.

In the communities in which we live, from a small band to a globe-inhabiting humanity, we have shown great capacity to connect, to share knowledge, and in a broader sense to benefit from belonging.

Through the multi-step transition from hunter-gatherer to farmer to factory worker to knowledge worker, we have become increasingly reliant on the social connections that support our endeavors. Before this transition we, as apex earth creatures, played a Win-Lose game.

Our early history was replete with stories of us winning and small game animals losing, saber-toothed tigers winning and us losing, the Ice Age winning and us losing, Neanderthals losing and Cro-Magnons winning. Our early history was essentially a story of kill or be killed, eat or be eaten in a one-on-one fight for survival.

Once we formed communities around agricultural plots, we relied more and more on each other for protection and to contribute and share in order to thrive, not just survive. In our modern, interconnected world, there is ample opportunity to turn the game into one of Win-Win.

The level of provision from the plurality, contributing and sharing in a synergistic effort, has been on a steady rise throughout the industrial age and into the information age. As a result, we now benefit from a modern world of free markets, free knowledge exchange, the freedom to search for truth, and the freedom to create and innovate, all of which have and will continue to open more doors to Win-Win opportunities.

Here are a few examples of Win-Win:

- Russia in space and America in space and global technology wins.
- A nation with abundant copper mining capacity but limited oil & gas production (Chile) exports copper to an oil-producing, copper-consuming counterpart (China).
- A pioneering electric car manufacturer, rather than patenting its innovative technology, shares it with competitors to seed a new market with volume necessary to prime overall demand.
- A company negotiates a lower price with a supplier in exchange for committing to a

larger order volume, ensuring both sides get a good deal.
- Two firms with non-competing but complementary products or services collaborate to reach new markets and customer segments.
- Participants in a civil suit secure a Win-Win settlement through mediation and good-faith negotiation rather than cutthroat, Machiavellian tactics.

Win-Win opportunities abound and are ripe for the picking for enterprising individuals and forward-thinking organizations. Much of the abundance and prosperity we enjoy today stems from our macro social structures, which enable us to connect, collaborate, and create more effectively.

Steven Covey, in his seminal book titled *7 Habits of Highly Effective People*, highlights Win-Win as one of his seven key success principles. The Win-Win mindset he describes is nurtured from an abundance mentality rather than from limiting beliefs of scarcity.

In his book, Mr. Covey explains how people with a Win-Win frame of mind "value cooperation over competition and believe that there is plenty of money, success, happiness, and good fortune to go around."

On the cautionary tale side of the story, he points out that "Leaders with the Win/Lose mentality use an authoritarian style of leadership; people with this mindset tend to use their authority, power, status, or personality to get what they want."

Modern technology enables Win-Win through trans-formational access to information and connected communication. It is our collective mindset, though, as it shifts towards a scarcity frame and cynicism, that must change to a positive one to fully benefit from Win-Win. The scarcity mindset manipulates us, pressuring us to become more materialistic, vain, prideful, less altruistic, and more selfish. With a greater divide between the 'haves' and the 'have-nots' in America, the battle lines between abundance and scarcity frames of mind are drawn.

...we now benefit from a modern world of free markets, free knowledge exchange, the freedom to search for truth, and the freedom to create and innovate, all of which have and will continue to open more doors to Win-Win opportunities.

We can be hopeful that an abundant mindset and associated Win-Win tactics will contribute to our safety, security, and a good deal of prosperity. Even though our technology and the ever-increasing scale of our social networks have helped us survive, prosper, and Win-Win more often, they have not been the prime agent for our self-perpetuation. It is the smaller social unit, the one bonded by blood and love —the family unit —that has long served this purpose.

The family is where nurturing, unconditional love and

a sense of belonging, destiny and legacy find a home. And it has been that way throughout history. It is where relationships are meant to flourish and endure and where we have traditionally sought to nurture our progeny. It has been the bedrock for our security and the centerpiece of our social hierarchies across not only centuries but millennia. The social power of family is indisputable. Arguably, strong families are the backbone of a cohesive and stable society.

The dynamics of the family unit, however, have changed significantly since the middle of the 20th century. There are many reasons for that change, but for now let's simply step back and reflect on what family life has looked like in America since the 1950s and ask ourselves if we are winning. Is Win-Win progressing or regressing within the confines of our most fundamental social unit, the family?

Questions to Ponder:

1. What new Win-Win scenarios can you create in your busy life to make a positive difference?
2. In what way can you counter the scarcity mindset and Win-Lose modus operandi of the people closest to you?

Chapter 5
Nuking the Family

Over the past 60 years, the average American family has evolved from the prototypical traditional nuclear family of the early 1960s, epitomized by the *Leave It to Beaver* Cleavers, to something much different. A traditional nuclear family consists of a married couple and their biological children who live at home with both parents. The Cleavers fit the mold of the time with a working father, a stay-at-home mother, and at least two kids living in the home.

The Cleaver parents were firm, fair, and caring with the father taking the lead in disciplining the children. The Cleavers regularly ate a home-cooked meal at home and attended church on Sundays. Today's family looks different. Firstly, fewer Americans choose to get married and have children. According to recent U.S. Census Bureau statistics, 34% of people 15 years or older had never been married in 2022. That's up from about 1 in 4 (23%) in 1950.

Additionally, fewer young American adults are opting to start a family. The overall birth rate in the United States has been declining for most of the past century and dropped by almost 23% between 2007 and 2022. In 1950, the average American woman had three children. Now she has about 1.6 children, which is well below the "replacement rate" of 2.1 children needed to maintain a stable population.

It has been said that to leave a legacy, one should write a book, plant a tree, or have children. It appears we have to write more books and plant more trees because we aren't having more children. Perhaps we are not as motivated nowadays to leave a family legacy, which is strange in that there seems to be an increasing interest lately in tracing and documenting one's ancestry in the form of a family tree. So, it appears that trees, whether of the verdant or family type, may be the key to legacy.

In efforts to establish themselves, young women have become more ambitious in their careers while men look to achieve some career success before settling down. This short-term focus, unfortunately, can create longer-term stress or sacrifice, particularly for women who want children but are running up against a biological clock.

Because raising a family can be a financial strain these days, many couples delay child rearing to focus on establishing a foundation, enjoying lifestyle flexibility and each other's company while building up savings as DINKs (double income no kids).

Once a modern couple becomes a family, though, it is likely that the widely different interests, disparate perspectives on life, and asymmetrical tech-based diversions change the daily routine. All this has led Jerry Seinfeld, as he does best, to find humor in reality, as he says, "There is no such thing as fun for the whole family." Perhaps the best that many families can do is to find fun in dysfunction.

Many adults do favor the traditional family approach, but overall, it seems that being a Cleaver is becoming passé. In the typical modern nuclear family, the father, mother, and children spend little quality time together. For example, the 1960's nightly ritual of eating at home together is now the exception not the norm.

Census data show other significant differences in family demographics over the past 60 years. Here are a couple of examples: Fewer people of age are married today. In 1960, 72% of adults over 18 were married, while today that number holds at just 51%. And for those folks who do get married, they are waiting longer to tie the knot. Throughout the 1960s, the median age for first-time brides was 20, and the median age for first-time grooms was 23. Today the median age for brides is 27; for grooms, it's 29.

Another American family lifestyle trend on the decline is church attendance. Well over 50% of families, including the Cleavers, regularly attended church each week in the 1960s. According to a Pew Research 'Religious Landscape Study' of February 2025, only 25% of adults reported that they and their families attended church weekly. One factor contributing to lower church attendance is the effort and logistics of attending church after a week of both parents being overwhelmed with caring for the children while working full-time jobs. Not taking the time, though, is a matter of priorities and priorities are driven by beliefs and values.

Clearly, the world today is vastly different from the 1960s, as lifestyles, economic environments, and societal norms and values have shifted away from traditional patterns. For example, in a break from the past, many kids today are choosing a path termed 'delayed adulthood' as they extend their teen lives into their late twenties, often living at home and breaking free of the nest as their social and work lives finally mature into adulthood by age 30. Ogden Nash once opined on a sad truth: "You are only young once, but you can stay immature indefinitely."

While all these trends reflect beliefs and choices that may seem beneficial to the individual in the short term, they are arguably not favorable to the welfare and sustainability of a healthy American family.

Families being less connected or being delayed in forming is one thing, but being broken is quite another. Another parenting trend that is not just weakening but breaking the family unit is parents who are missing in action. In 1968, 85% of children under the age of 18 lived with two parents. By 2020, that number had dropped significantly to 70%, with 80% of these single-parent households headed by women. Furthermore, in 1980, approximately 18% of all women who gave birth were unmarried, while in 2021 that number had risen to 40%.

While all these trends reflect beliefs and choices that may seem beneficial to the individual in the short term, they are arguably not favorable to the welfare and sustainability of a healthy American family.

We now have a demographic landscape overpopulated with fractured families, where children grow up without a father. The adverse effect upon a child growing up without a father figure is well documented. Children in father-absent homes are:

- Almost four times more likely to be poor.
- Show higher levels of aggressive behavior than children born to married mothers. (U.S. Census Bureau)
- Are facing unprecedented uncertainty, experiencing elevated stress and reporting symptoms of depression. (Journal of Marriage and Family)
- Are more likely to abuse drugs and alcohol. (Stress in America 2020: A National Mental Health Crisis)
- Are more likely to be influenced by negative adult male role models and, in the process, drop out of school and get involved in criminal activity more often than kids in two-parent homes. (Social Science Research)

The slow disintegration of the family which exiles our youth into a disadvantaged environment poses a real threat to normalcy and prosperity in America. Weak social environments tend to produce weak young adults.

Troubling Signs of a Dysfunctional Family:

1. There is no honest, healthy communication
2. Conditional love reigns supreme
3. There is little or no discipline
4. Children rarely bring friends home
5. Constant conflict: days are fraught with drama
6. Family members disown each other
7. The holidays are not joyful
8. Unresolved conflict and tension run rampant
9. Role reversal with kids forced into parenting
10. Excessive secrecy and controlling behaviors

Questions to Ponder:

1. How can you help create a healthier home environment for you and your family?
2. In what ways are your relationships outside of family (other than life partner) stronger, deeper, and more meaningful than within your family?

Part 3

Belonging in Today's World

Chapter 6
Wimpification

From helicopter parents to the enticing and hypnotic allure of social media to the fracturing of the nuclear family, our younger generations have been dealt a bad hand. The coddling, the special privileges, the cushy environment in which they live have made them entitled to the point of being wimpy. Yes, we are guilty of indoctrinating our kids into the world of wimpiness.

The wimpification (to coin a new term) of our kids has stripped them of the personal fortitude required to become responsible human beings. We tend to squelch the adventuresome, curious, and daring nature that our kids exude immediately upon toddlerhood. Children learn about the big world by creating their own small personal worlds. Toddlers delight in having agency in their personal space – having fun seeing that their actions can cause noise, objects to move or other changes brought about by their simple but bold cause/effect experiments.

Unfortunately, the bold and daring aspects of being a kid are often stripped away through overparenting. The free-range kids of yesterday are gone and are now replaced by fragile, needy kids who over-rely on their parents and grow up late and often only partially.

For many kids who do have a father in their life, their wimpification is exacerbated by a weakening of that father figure. The days of the rugged, stoic, and disciplined 'Marlboro Man' are gone. The image of men, the fathers of our kids, the traditional head of the family, is increasingly tilted towards a meek, soft, and submissive persona. The macho, the tough, the strong, the firm but fair male image is on the wane. Factors contributing to this decline include the empowerment of women, confusion of gender roles, and media depiction of the typical American dad.

The noble cause of the women's liberation movement of the late 1900s was to elevate women and celebrate the idea that they have the right and ability to achieve their full potential. Over the past twenty years, the new age women's movement has become more adversarial, with bashing men a common battle cry and modus operandi. Furthermore, the current unravelling of traditional roles of the sexes and the related gender fluidity running rampant confuses the whole issue of what a man is or should be.

A traditional strong and capable man is driven to seek an adventuresome life that tests his mettle. Cultural conditioning, though, often puts up barriers blocking his inherent instincts.

When stepping into his traditional male persona, the

modern American male risks being perceived as a stooge of toxic masculinity. Speaking of stooges, it is clear that mainstream media has a penchant for portraying men, particularly fathers, as bumbling, misanthropic dolts, much like Al Bundy of *Married with Children* and Homer Simpson of *The Simpsons*.

Unfortunately, as is becoming ever more evident, when society lashes out at masculinity, we don't get stronger men; we don't get heroes; we either have men retreat and acquiesce weakly or we see them metamorphose into dangerous agents lashing out against the world at large, upending relationships as they rebel.

One strong and accomplished man, an antithesis of a wimp, Arnold Schwarzenegger, in an interview with Howard Stern in October of 2023, harped on the subject of wimpiness. You know Arnold, the Austrian Oak who won the world's top bodybuilding title seven times, rose to fame as a Hollywood icon, and later became governor of California.

In his interview, Arnold doled out advice to parents, encouraging them to counter the trend toward fragility and wimpiness, saying, "It's nice to be considerate, yes. I totally agree with that. But let's not overprotect the kids. Let's go and teach kids to be tough, to go out and do sports, to study, to struggle, you know, to go through these kinds of painful moments sometimes. It's just the way it is. You have to be able to struggle. You can only strengthen your character, become a really strong person inside, if you have resistance — if you fail, if you get up again, and if you work hard."

Agreed, Arnold, we need more real men and tough

and resilient offspring. We could use a resurgence of courage and grit and a healthy dose of stoicism to fight against the wimpy movement that is underfoot. Charlie Kirk often voiced this same sentiment on college campuses saying that it is more important for our kids to grow up with self-control than with self-esteem.

Unfortunately, the norm is for kids, deleteriously coddled, summarily abandoned, or suffering from a lack of a strong male influence, to grow up through adolescence into college age, confused and conditioned to being weak and wimpy. We teach them to tune into their feelings and never to question their emotions, in effect, to be not the master of their emotions but their slave.

In their wimpiness, as they suffer from an incurable impotence, our young adult kids attempt to assuage the pain by pointing fingers of blame toward the patriarchy, systemic prejudice, injustice embedded in institutions, as well as whatever economic ills they feel capitalism lays at their feet. This weakness of spirit has the masses of our young adults wallow in their wimpiness, having succumbed to the enticing narrative of victimhood that is energized and hardened into their psyche.

Pain particularly when self-inflicted has a way of consuming the soul. On the other hand, mentally tough individuals who endure and remain steadfast in the face of deep, externally imposed pain, often emerge with the strongest purpose.

If you are having trouble identifying the wimp inside of you or others then reflect on whether these weak victim-centric emotions have taken root: envy, jealousy, contempt, anger, resentment, and shame. As appalling as it may seem, these wimpified victim states of mind are amplified at the indoctrination camps we call college campuses.

When our kids begin their time in college, they are encouraged to play the victim card. On college campuses, they rally to ban visitors from speaking on sensitive topics because the expected content is feared to be threatening.

Why are they so afraid of discussing their beliefs in a civilized manner?

Those same students often revolt in the face of any perceived 'micro-aggressions' and if those tactics fail, they complain and seek solace and protection in 'safe spaces.' Kowtowing to their frailties, we have now invented a solution even for these micro-aggressions, these innocuous transgressions of subtle expressions or actions deemed unmitigatedly dangerous. The solution is to issue a trigger warning, which signals in advance any little thing that might upset impressionable minds.

This weakness of spirit has the masses of our young adults wallow in their wimpiness, having succumbed to the enticing narrative of victimhood that is energized and hardened into their psyche.

It seems as though we have produced a new generation of young adults who are overly sensitive, fragile, and prone to endless complaining. Indeed, a new word has been added to the lexicon to describe the specialness and frailty of our progeny. That term 'snowflake', as in snowflake generation, was added officially to both the *Collins Dictionary* and the *Oxford English Dictionary* between 2016 and 2018. At the same time, the *Financial Times* included snowflake in their Year in a Word list defining it as: "A derogatory term for someone deemed too emotionally vulnerable to cope with views that challenge their own, particularly in universities and other forums once known for robust debate."

Snowflakes, the kind made of real snow, are unique or special and wilt and melt when exposed to heat. Wimps are patently the same.

Questions to Ponder:

1. What actions can you take to become more responsible, determined and purposeful in your pursuits?
2. In what ways might you become a positive influence or role model, motivating others to invest in stronger relationships and more productive endeavors?

Society is built not through the feeble attempts of the isolated and weak, but through strong, action-oriented individuals in supportive relationships. Relationships forged on the foundation of integrity and trust are what harness the energy and power of society's difference makers.

Let's take a closer look at the state of today's relationships to answer the following questions:

How are today's most important relationships shifting over time?

Which relationships have slackened, which ones continue to hold court, and which ones are on the rise in modern America?

Are the shifts in relationships contributing to societal progress or triggering societal regression?

Chapter 7

Relationship 4 F's

Our socialization, at least in our formative years, primarily takes root within the family unit. As discussed earlier, the nuclear family has weakened over the past few decades. Family has traditionally been the home to many of our most important relationships as a parent, life partner, child, or sibling. As deep personal connections are essential, is it possible that family ties are losing out to other connections for our most valued relationships?

With the decline in religiosity since the late 1900s, it's fair to say that the search for deep relationships has not been drawing people to God. If it's not in God or family where we pursue our most valued relationships, where is it?

Clearly, friends are among the most important relationships in our lives. According to a summer 2023 Pew Research Center survey, 61% of U.S. adults say that close friendships are extremely or very important for living a fulfilling life. This is far greater than those who say the same about wanting marriage (23%), children (26%) or a lot of money (24%). Wanting and having, though, are two different things.

A Google search for "the state of friendship in America" returns responses including:

- Americans have fewer friends than ever before
- Why Americans are spending less time with friends
- Why America is suffering from a Friendship Recession

A related search will return results from the NORC @ The University of Chicago 'General Social Survey on Neighbor Socialization'. The survey found that many Americans do not make friends with their real-life neighbors, and by 2015, nearly one in three Americans reported not socializing with their neighbors.

With traditional relationships and religiosity on the wane, where are we, as social animals, searching for connection?

Yes, it's on social platforms where the majority now invest significant time and energy in relationships. Unfortunately, virtual relationships are at best self-serving and at worst insincere and manipulative. Online, we are obsessed with ourselves, our image, and our looks, with a prime objective of garnering attention, likes, and followers. This obsession has us more infatuated with the social cred that comes with building a cadre of followers or virtual friends than with genuine relationships with our parents, families, or real neighbors.

Our relationships are defined to some degree by how we greet and acknowledge each other. Before the internet, we often followed the advice of Dale Carnegie, who suggested, "A person's name is to that person the sweetest and most important sound in any language." With caller ID and text messaging automatically identifying both parties, there is little motive nowadays to address others by name. You may have noticed that our younger generations carry this programming into their daily lives, rarely greeting casual acquaintances by name.

It appears we only care about getting noticed, building followers, or even going viral for our 15 minutes of fame, rather than investing in mutually beneficial relationships built on empathy and love. There is little love shared on (X)Twitter, and the interactions on the other social platforms often cause collateral damage in the form of FOMO anxiety, bullying of opposing camps, and, most venomously, attacks on targeted individuals.

Over time, the Relationship 4 F's have evolved from traditional to exhibitionist and artificial. We have shifted from valuing meaningful and long-lasting relationships with family and real friends as the center of our social universe to valuing shallow, selfish virtual relationships that can, at best, manifest in likes and followers.

As the graphic below illustrates, the emphasis we place on each of the Relationship 4F's has devolved over time. From warriors to self-absorbed wimps, we have transitioned from living fully and fighting the battles of real-world purpose, strengthened by family and friends, to retreating into the comforting confines of a narcissistic, instantly gratifying virtual world that measures significance by something as unimportant as the number of followers.

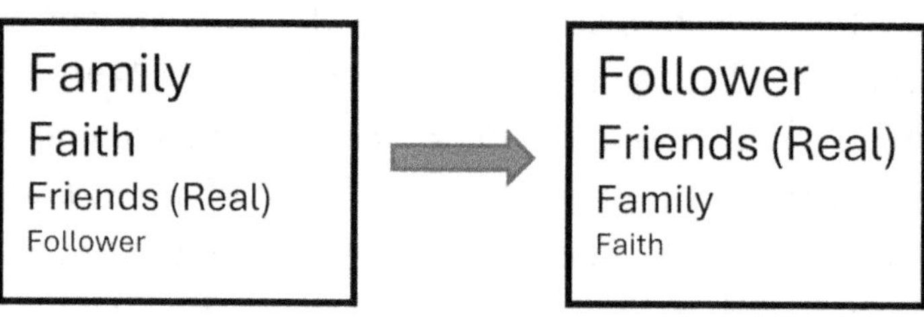

We have shifted from valuing meaningful and long-lasting relationships with family and real friends as the center of our social universe to valuing shallow, selfish virtual relationships that can, at best, manifest in likes and followers.

Questions to Ponder:

1. How can you shift your 4F priorities to better enable long-term fulfillment for you and the most important people in your life?
2. What is an easy first step you can take to get unstuck from a misplaced 4F priority?

Here's something to think about. The Relationship 4F's have been turned upside down with online community status being revered. Is that pursuit merely a game played in pursuit of belonging or is it affecting us more deeply, in terms of the people we are becoming?

Chapter 8
Victimhood and Crybabies

When life doesn't go your way and you're too much of a wimp or snowflake to step up to make a positive difference, the one recourse in attempting to gain some semblance of significance is to complain or play out provocative power-striving machinations. That propensity to complain has now been supercharged through our 21st-century solution for fostering connectedness –social media platforms.

The social platforms, including Facebook, X, Instagram, and TikTok, have become playgrounds for hyperbole and for outrageous, downright shocking shenanigans. The more edgy, the more provocative, the better. Extremists have taken over.

These social playgrounds are lucrative and self-perpetuating, as there is social cred and even financial reward for those who dare to be outlandish enough to grab a significant amount of attention. These extremely popular global social platforms inundate their audience with a profusion of posts, all vying for attention. Unfortunately, it is vengeful and vicious verbal attacks as well as perverse and provocative content that capture attention and attract a larger audience.

As more and more tune in, the viral fame, followers, and influence can be parlayed into subscriptions or sponsorships and the copious amounts of money that can flow from that. Indeed, millions tune in and are hooked by the social platforms' beckoning call.

Along with edgy content, underlying messages that stir significant emotion can commandeer attention amid the online chaos. Misery loves company. It is there where the wimps have their forum to be crybabies, and the crybabies love to bellyache and moan in their one big playpen.

Online victims come together to whine about common struggles and to gripe about how bad things are. The typical refrain is that society's problems are the fault of opposing individuals or groups. Indeed, there is a lot of complaining and finger-pointing online, which tends to pit the perceived oppressed versus their oppressors.

The victims, the crybaby complainers among us, play this game best, and it is our young, our most tech-dependent demographic, who are being indoctrinated into the sanctum of victimhood.

The online victims, to garner attention, work hard to convince the virtual world that their suffering is unmatched in the land of oppression. These social media crybabies love to share evidence of their unfair treatment while in the process lambasting the Machiavellian methods of the victimizers, who, in turn, reject the accusations.

So now we see victims of various degrees of mistreatment and their victimizers all preoccupied with laying the strongest claim to being mistreated, manipulated, or verbally attacked. Within the ranks of the victims and into the armies of the oppressors is a twisted predilection to picking a fight in the arena of an Oppression Olympics.

Along with edgy content, underlying messages that stir significant emotion can commandeer attention amid the online chaos. Misery loves company.

Because claims of oppression are stronger with more voices and because mob psychology can help enlist a cadre of sympathizers, those who feel victimized tend to identify with a group, so that collectively their grievances can carry more clout. This creates division across many dimensions, pitting one extreme view and group against polar opposite views and groups. Centrist opinions aren't valued much online. If you want to enter the fray, you have no choice but to enlist in one extreme faction or the other.

Hmm... has social media made us more anti-social?

Does contrived belongingness manifest most strongly in the virtual world?

Are the social platforms antithetical to genuine connection?

The Oppression Olympics is organized so that participants battle under their own unique and defining flag. Over time, this division online widens further as clickbait and provocative content push the conversation ever further onto the fringe.

In the combat arena, it devolves to a fight between the remaining players, the extremists, who carry all the clout and who conspire to exercise a tyranny of the minority. It indeed is a tyranny, as the oppressed and their virtue-signaling sponsors often go to drastic measures to retaliate for the oppression of favored minorities.

When whim strikes, they attack, ridicule, and cancel perpetrators, banishing them from the field of play as they unleash the fury of 'Cancel Culture'. The canceling in the arena is reminiscent of Roman emperors being encouraged by the crowd to brandish their thumbs of justice to forever silence the offender.

In the online battlefield, where entertainment is a key factor, it is a perpetual fight for social status. There, the combatants seek first to win the battle by combining voices with comrades. Soon, though, the skirmishes escalate to attacking the other side, which incites higher levels of aggression and division.

It is worth noting, and quite sad, that all these daily online skirmishes, the Oppression Olympics, tend to be primed mostly by bombastic arguments about trivial daily news. In the giant Olympic coliseum of the internet, all the pageantry, ceremony, and yes, acrimony, is almost always about nothing!

The modern platforms serve up greater visibility of the daily news cycle, and that yields continuous fodder for arguing of banal and boisterous blather.

From obsessing and arguing over interpretation of optical illusions (is the dress blue or gold), to being endlessly entertained by dangerous and just plain stupid challenges including, The Coke and Mentos Challenge, The Car Surfing Challenge, the outright life-threatening challenge of eating Tide Pods and more, to elevating all kinds of trivial new items of the day into attempts to gain online views and peer validation, should have us think - Get a grip! Get a life! Grow up!

Troubling Signs of Online Addiction*

Have you noticed how in our digital world folks are:

1. Continuously tethered to a personal cell phone
2. Controlled by a severe itch to look at a screen with every notice ping
3. Sending and receiving daily text messages numbering in the dozens
4. Suffering from sleep deprivation due to spending time online late at night
5. Using the internet to alter mood, deal with anxiety, and stress
6. Venting with anger when internet access is not available

7. Getting caught up in videogame, gambling or sexual content obsession
8. Using the social platforms to find significance

Internet addiction disorder (IAD) is a real thing

It seems that most online aficionados are devolving into ignorant adolescent versions of their adult selves. One can take solace, though, that eventually, these online combatants will realize they are fighting mostly with emotional rantings about temporary, non-strategic, and ephemeral events that have no real significance.

In the meantime, to legitimize their rantings and extreme views, online adolescents attempt to connect the dots of several news items to weave together a supposed story of strategic substance, crafting the grand conspiracy theory of the week. The conspiracy theories resonate with complainers, victims, and emotion-fueled arbiters of truth, despite seldom, if ever, holding up to rational scrutiny and invariably succumbing to reasoned logic. But that is OK, as there is always another conspiracy to spin upon the demise of the other.

The cycle of victimhood for the crybabies in the online complaining camps perpetuates and continues to satiate a desperate need for attention and significance. It is this desperation that mutates helpless victims into full-fledged crybabies who demand instant relief from their perceived pain. The crybaby's modus operandi is to focus on emotion, biased opinion, hapless appeals for significance, and excuses posited as being a victim of oppression. But all of that comes up short.

There is a bigger void that begs to be filled. An absence of knowledge, purpose, and true connectedness that would otherwise be the basis for meaning, belongingness, and a fulfilling life.

The wimps, who we allow to complain like crybabies, are on a trajectory of limited awareness and a lack of knowledge of the world and one's purpose in it. The wimps-turned-crybabies are now evolving into dummies.

Questions to Ponder:

1. In what ways has the divisiveness of modern society infiltrated your daily life?
2. In what ways do you feel penalized for being truly authentic today?

Part 4

Who We Are Becoming

Chapter 9

Dummies and the Mentally Weak

Playing the crybaby game requires no education, historical knowledge, or appreciation for the institutions that built a prosperous society. As a result, today's dummies take the easy way out by fabricating false stories of history and truth, and outsourcing their thinking ('Alexa, do this' or 'Siri, what is...?'). When they do their own thinking, they often expose themselves to criticism, so they become more provocative while using fewer facts.

The old saying about remaining silent to avoid proving yourself a fool is regularly ignored online.

Our younger generations now resort to vitriol instead of debate, working to silence anyone who disagrees with them - on college campuses, online, or by canceling. They're not just squelching free speech but also stifling free thinking and knowledge-building. College and high schools are fertile ground for the indoctrination of wimpy, crybaby thoughts and behaviors.

In his May 2023 article published in *The Free Press* titled "At High School Debates, Debate is No Longer Allowed," James Fishback, a veteran debate coach, says he has seen a decline in high school debate from a forum that rewards evidence and reasoning to one that punishes students for what they say.

Fishback argues against criticism of words not 'politically correct' by saying, "Should a high school student automatically lose and be publicly humiliated for using a term that's not only ubiquitous in media and politics, but accurate? Unfortunately for students and their parents, there are countless judges at tournaments across the country whose biased paradigms disqualify them from being impartial adjudicators of debate. During my time as a coach, I witnessed many students lose interest and drop out. They'd had enough of being told what they could and couldn't say."

Fishback voices a legitimate concern. Our First Amendment right to free speech is being challenged in the places where future generations are being educated. This squelching of free speech is rooted in the victim-centric, wimpy, and fragile belief that one's right not to be offended trumps another's right to free speech. Our Founding Fathers, including Thomas Paine, Ben Franklin, George Washington, and Thomas Jefferson, would be appalled.

Our younger generations now resort to vitriol instead of debate, working to silence anyone who disagrees with them - on college campuses, online, or by canceling.

Are We Actually Getting Dumber?

Are we truly becoming dumber year by year, or is it just our imagination? Is healthy truth-seeking debate now becoming obsolete since we can't call a spade a spade? Is there no tolerance for opposing opinions or valuing of cognitive ability or mental agility? Is common sense not so common anymore?

The evidence suggests, yes. Let's explore this dumbing-down question intellectually by reviewing a couple of studies on the subject.

Intelligence levels, as gauged by our best measure, IQ, increased through the 20th century. This trend was documented by James Flynn, a New Zealand-based intelligence researcher, and dubbed the 'Flynn Effect.' But surprisingly, the most comprehensive study on the subject, conducted on 750,000 Norwegian men (1962 – 1991), showed that the Flynn Effect began to reverse around 1975. Since then, IQ dropped roughly 7 points per generation.

A study at Northwestern University analyzed intelligence testing data comparing intelligence levels from 2006 to 2018 for 400,000 Americans. It showed declines in <u>three out of four</u> cognitive categories: verbal reasoning, matrix reasoning, and mathematical abilities. Only spatial reasoning has improved, perhaps due to our regular exposure to realistic 3D images in computer interfaces and gaming software.

Scientists point to multiple culprits: a poorer diet, changes in our educational systems, a decline in reading and writing skills, attention deficit disorder driven by internet-driven data overload, and social media obsession. A study at the University of Texas at Austin found that people retain information better when their smartphones are in another room. Epiphany: our phones are becoming smarter, while we are not.

According to 2024 results from the National Assessment of Educational Progress (NAEP), often referred to as 'the nation's report card', average reading and math scores among 12th graders fell to their <u>lowest levels on record</u>. Lesley Muldoon, executive director of the National Assessment Governing Board, says, "Students are taking their next steps in life with fewer skills and less knowledge in core academics than their predecessors a decade ago." Ms. Muldoon adds, "This is happening when rapid advancements in technology and society demand more of future workers and citizens, not less."

Jonathan Haidt, a social psychologist at the NYU Stern School of Business, made a compelling claim in his April 11, 2022, article in *The Atlantic* titled "Why the past 10 years of American life have been uniquely stupid...It's not just a phase." He speaks to the psychological impact laid down by the major social media platforms, saying in part, "The most pervasive obstacle to good thinking is confirmation bias, which refers to the human tendency to search only for evidence that confirms our preferred beliefs.

Even before the advent of social media, the algorithm-driven search engines were supercharging confirmation bias, making it far easier for people to find evidence for absurd beliefs and conspiracy theories, such as that the Earth is flat and that the U.S. government staged the 9/11 attacks. But social media made things much worse."

Haidt further points to Twitter's retweet feature and Facebook's share button, which amplified confirmation bias and mob dynamics. "One of the engineers at Twitter who had worked on the retweet button later revealed that he regretted his contribution because it had made Twitter a nastier place. As he watched Twitter mobs forming through the use of the new tool, he thought to himself, "We might have just handed a 4-year-old a loaded weapon.'"

The dumbing down has reached a whole new level of pervasiveness as key institutions, including universities, creative industries, and political organizations, have traded intelligence for dogma due to a chronic fear of being ostracized, disenfranchised, or, in simple current-day terms, canceled. Canceling is mandated to extol any point of view that counters the current, often extreme and simplistic narrative.

Because of the protective veil of anonymity on social platforms, the dumbness proliferates to outlandish proportions online. Echo chambers create powerful psychological forces and social pressures, keeping the narrative curated and, as a result, increasingly dumb.

What we call dumbing down might be better characterized as a deterioration of mental strength—the ability to manage thoughts, emotions, and behaviors responsibly and productively, even in challenging situations. One can argue that it is not just our intellectual smarts but also our mental strength (the wisdom of how best to thrive in our world) that seem to be tracking in the wrong direction.

Reflect on whether the following ideas are true: The more information that we have the less we seem to understand. We confuse noise for signal, awareness for comprehension, repetition for validity, opinion for fact, and knowledge for wisdom.

Now that you're in thinking mode, mull this over. Are key virtues of mental strength, such as self-awareness, growth and abundance mindsets, emotional intelligence, adaptability, resilience, temperance, and courage, being degraded as our collective intelligence regresses?

Consider emotional intelligence (EQ): the capacity to be aware of, control, and express one's emotions, and to handle interpersonal relationships judiciously and empathetically. Daniel Goleman identified four EQ domains: Self-awareness, Self-management, Social Awareness, and Relationship Management. Unlike IQ, EQ is uniquely human – AI has no equivalent.

How are we humans doing on the EQ front? Not well.

In a survey across demographic groups, Six Seconds – The Emotional Intelligence Network published findings on global EQ trends in their study "State of the Heart

2024: New Data on Emotional Intelligence, Wellbeing and the Emotional Recession." They found that global emotional intelligence scores have declined each year from 2019 to 2023, resulting in a total decline of more than 5.5% over the period.

The world has entered an 'emotional recession', characterized by low well-being and high burnout—a condition decades in the making, but alarmingly accelerating now.

10 Symptoms of Mental Strength Deficit

Have you seen folks who...?

1. Expect immediate results
2. Feel entitled to privileges
3. Crave external validation
4. Waste energy on things they can't control
5. Struggle to live in the present
6. Let prejudices or biases cloud their critical thinking
7. Get ensnared by gossip or conspiracy theories
8. Let others limit their joy

Living with these kinds of deficits sabotages success by stimulating all the wrong behavior. But here's the kicker: because mental strength is common sense – reasoning and doing what we know is right – our problem isn't purely intelligence. It's a wimpy nature, a lack of personal fortitude or courage that greenlights harmful routines and detrimental conduct. As we become wimpy, we increasingly find ourselves among the mentally weak and underachieving.

OK, so our mental strength appears to be on the decline. Despite that trend, have we remained optimistic about the future and happy in our current circumstances? The next chapter should help answer that question.

Questions to Ponder:

1. What opinions and judgments do you hear being voiced repeatedly despite a lack of factual evidence?
2. What have you experienced that has you feel that with most people, feelings matter more than the truth?

Chapter 10

Fat, Dumb, and Unhappy

The dumbing down of America, primed by online influence and accelerated by family breakdown and failing schools, is weakening our future generations. We have cheated our children out of a healthy, family-centered development.

Standardized tests prove that schools are failing them academically. And with church attendance declining, many kids don't have that stabilizing place outside the home that protects them against the often-misguided thought programming and moral deconditioning that can occur in the classroom.

With schools not doing what they used to do to help kids mature into responsible and capable adults, our young people seek out social platforms as a place of refuge.

Unfortunately, the refuge is, in reality, refuse, aka garbage! Aggressively promoted fake livestyles induce FOMO (fear of missing out), bullying, and division. Kids don't learn real-life lessons online. They struggle enough in school, and overprotective parents often rob them of the opportunity to learn through experience. They learn the wrong lessons from social platforms. No wonder their mental capacities are stunted by college age.

The divisive nature of the social platform world is no place for a kid to grow up. From there, more aggressive reprogramming of their impressionable young minds leads our young adults to question not only their own worthiness but also that of our country and institutions.

Their belief systems are being hijacked. Schools indoctrinate rather than educate. It seems that everyone or every group has a self-serving and partisan agenda.

With schools not doing what they used to do to help kids mature into responsible and capable adults, our young people seek out social platforms as a place of refuge.

Meanwhile, mainstream media and social platforms serve attention-grabbing bad news. In their unstable world, kids retreat to their pacifier – their cell phone – for fleeting relief. For chronic conditions, when purpose, meaning, and fulfillment remain distant, the coping mechanism of choice is victimhood. Incessantly playing the part of victim in a loser game, though, can easily become a relentless mental strain and soul-stressing endeavor.

Our youth could benefit from the advice from Rocky Balboa , "You, me, or nobody is gonna hit as hard as life. But it ain't about how hard you hit. It's about how hard you can get hit and keep moving forward; how much you can take and keep moving forward. That's how winning is done!" You got that right, Rocky! Winning beats losing any day. Being a victor trumps being a victim every single day.

Unfortunately, though, many of us are fighting a losing battle. In a 2015 report titled "An Epidemic of Anguish," published by the Chronicle of Higher Education, it was found that one fourth of college students presented diagnosable mental illness symptoms, including classical manifestations of anxiety and depression. Suicide rates amongst students were three times higher than it was in 1950.

Frustration, fear, and growing dissatisfaction with life are tough battles to fight alone. Our kids, many of whom are lost, distressed, and searching for meaning, invariably turn to social platforms to seek validation from others, convincing themselves of their own worthiness.

Failing to connect and form genuine human relationships, the intrepid idealists fall further into victimhood. They lash out, projecting their troubles on others, feeling justified based on having suffered through a pampered yet unfulfilled upbringing that gives them the right to complain, and complain they do.

It's not just our kids; most of us use social platform groups and forums to bitch and moan and to take sides on any issue, which leads to ever more fracturing of families and communities. A cushy life creates entitled, self-centered wimps who become crybabies online, then dummies, searching for validation from strangers. Social media addiction is having a pernicious effect: we're evolving into a country of wimps, crybabies, and dummies.

We are becoming dummies, ignorant of history, dismissive of rational thought, incapable of level-headed social discourse, and bereft of purpose. Is it a surprise that young professionals entering the workforce are apt to complain about and have difficulty adjusting to a nine-to-five routine while insisting that their employer's company give them a sense of purpose? Is it a surprise that workers today between the ages of 25 and 34 hold a job for an average of 2.8 years?

Humans are hardwired to thrive in caring and supportive relationships, both socially and in their personal and professional lives. The family and faith connections that have been so instrumental in the past are now devalued. Our younger generations are struggling, as if they are in the desert, frantically searching for refreshment, connection, and purpose, only to have the oasis of social media come up dry with few recognizing it as a mirage. It hasn't always been this way.

Around 2000, we could have described many Americans as fat, dumb, and happy – naïve about hard truths. Overconsumption and the lure of instant gratification made us fat. Compare beach pictures from the 1970s with those taken in the past 20 years, and you will have ample evidence of the increasing prevalence of obesity in our population. We grew fatter and dumber indulging in our advantaged lifestyle, and we were happy because the social inequities and ungodliness of our world hid behind a curtain.

Nicholas H. Wolfinger documented the 1990 happiness highwater mark in his "Trends in Young Adult Happiness: 1990 to 2022", published Dec. 12, 2023, by the Institute for Family Studies. In 1990, Wolfinger cites survey results showing that 36% of Americans aged 18-35 reported being very happy.

The happiness measure dropped to 28% over the following 25 years, and then again to below 20% during the COVID years. The 1990s were our "blue pill" moment – to borrow from *The Matrix* – where ignorance was bliss and we believed what we wanted to believe.

But then things changed. A red pill world soon emerged.

After the dot.com bubble, 9/11, the 2008 recession, and the World Series win by the Chicago Cubs in 2016, our state of mind had awakened to a new red pill existence; a glitch in the matrix, a normalcy-shattering reality, and a plight of agitation we can call 'Fat, Dumb, and Unhappy.'

The internet and social media platforms shattered our naiveté by pulling the curtain back showing us startling, streamed videos and sensationalized news. Seeing what our blinders had previously covered up, we now feel left out, as if we don't measure up, are victimized, and woefully unhappy. It was Theodore Roosevelt who said, "Comparison is the thief of joy." Joy is waning...

With blinders off, the increasingly cushy existence has forged a society that enables wimps, encourages them to be crybabies, and provides no incentive to be anything other than a dummy.

True to form, dummies arrive with twisted thinking, limited knowledge, and disempowering beliefs. Wimps carry themselves feebly, lack courage and are easily discouraged. Crybabies exacerbate it all by imposing a grumbling and griping backdrop of complaints, immaturity, and unconstrained emotion.

Despite folks becoming increasingly wimpy, whiny, and wacky is there still hope for a prosperous future? Or are the personality foibles a sign of deeper despair?

Questions to Ponder:

1. What steps will you take to rid yourself of wimpy, dumb, and crybaby behavior?
2. How can you help a young person become more mentally strong, broadly capable, and genuinely fulfilled?

Chapter 11

War on the American Dream

Yes, it's dire. Many indicators point to a downward trajectory where the American Dream is out of reach where we've become fractured, distracted and aimless while trading rational dialogue for crybaby complaints and wimpy behavior.

Much of what is transpiring in society was prophesied 60 years ago by Paul Harvey, a well-known radio personality. In 1965, Paul Harvey broadcasted "If I Were the Devil." Here is a transcript from that radio broadcast:

"If I were the devil ... If I were the Prince of Darkness, I'd want to engulf the whole world in darkness. And I'd have a third of its real estate, and four-fifths of its population, but I wouldn't be happy until I had seized the ripest apple on the tree — Thee. So, I'd set about, however necessary, to take over the United States. I'd subvert the churches first — I'd begin with a campaign of

whispers. With the wisdom of a serpent, I would whisper to you as I whispered to Eve: 'Do as you please'.

To the young, I would whisper, 'The Bible is a myth.' I would convince them that man created God instead of the other way around. I would confide that what's bad is good, and what's good is 'square.' And the old, I would teach to pray, after me, 'Our Father, which art in Washington... And then I'd get organized.

I'd educate authors in how to make lurid literature exciting, so that anything else would appear dull and uninteresting. I'd threaten TV with dirtier movies and vice versa. I'd peddle narcotics to whom I could. I'd sell alcohol to ladies and gentlemen of distinction. I'd tranquilize the rest with pills.

If I were the devil, I'd soon have families at war with themselves, churches at war with themselves, and nations at war with themselves, until each in its turn was consumed. And with promises of higher ratings, I'd have mesmerizing media fanning the flames. If I were the devil, I would encourage schools to refine young intellects but neglect to discipline emotions — just let those run wild until, before you knew it, you'd have to have drug sniffing dogs and metal detectors at every schoolhouse door.

Within a decade, I'd have prisons overflowing, I'd have judges promoting pornography — soon I could evict God from the courthouse, then from the schoolhouse, and then from the houses of Congress. And in His own churches, I would substitute psychology for religion and deify science. I would lure priests and pastors into misusing boys and girls, and church money.

If I were the devil, I'd make the symbol of Easter an egg and the symbol of Christmas a bottle. If I were the devil, I'd take from those who have, and give to those who want, until I had killed the incentive of the ambitious.

And what do you bet I could get whole states to promote gambling as the way to get rich? I would caution against extremes and hard work in Patriotism, in moral conduct. I would convince the young that marriage is old-fashioned, that swinging is more fun, and that what you see on TV is the way to be. And thus, I could undress you in public, and I could lure you into bed with diseases for which there is no cure. In other words, if I were the devil, I'd just keep right on doing what he's doing.
~Paul Harvey, good day."

Wow! Does that have a familiar feel? Does Paul Harvey's 60-year-old vision read like common-sense observations of trends playing out right now? It should.

Is a dark, dysfunctional future looming? Are we watching the social fabric unravel in ways long envisioned? Can we step up to the challenge to climb out of the wimpy, crybaby, dummy doldrums we're in? With things spiraling ever faster, is it time for real solutions?

Now is a good time for a little introspection into the best that lies within us and whether that potential is threatened, thwarted, or just waiting to be ignited. First, before we pull on that potential, we must recover from the downward slide caused by Internet addiction disorder and the afflictions and hardships related to Convenience Culture and the upending of the Relationship 4 F's.

To create a better future, we should examine the mechanisms that are shaping our society, with technology as the priming force. Beyond technology, seven related trends form a weapon aimed at the heart of the American Dream – at our sense of normalcy, prosperity, and hope.

Let's examine where we are now and connect the dots on the dispiriting forces of today.

Questions to Ponder:

1. What opportunities can you pursue to progress toward your American Dream?
2. How can you help a special person achieve their American Dream?

Part 5

Societal Shapers of Today

Chapter 12

Technology

The methods, systems, and devices
resulting from scientific knowledge
applied for practical purposes.

ABC News

*Instagram imposes new restrictions for teens.
Will they work?* By Max Zahn September 18, 2024

"Instagram this week unveiled mandatory accounts for teens that bolster privacy protections, enable parental supervision, and restrict notifications during overnight hours. New and existing users under the age of 18 will be automatically enrolled in what Instagram is calling "Teen Accounts," the company said.

The move comes 16 months after U.S. Surgeon General Vivek Murthy warned in an advisory that excessive social media could pose a "profound risk" to the mental health of children. Instagram also has faced pressure from some federal and state lawmakers seeking to regulate social media use among children and teens."

Science and technology have pioneered remarkable advancements throughout history. The movable-type printing press in the 15th century accelerated the dissemination of knowledge and spread enlightening ideas across Europe. Since then, communication has advanced through the telephone, radio, television, computer, internet, and mobile phones – each drastically reshaping society.

Historically the reshaping forged by technology came so fast that many parts of our communities struggled to adjust. For example, the steam engine enabled railroads and industrialization, displacing agrarian communities and accelerating urbanization. Nuclear fission created the atomic bomb and mutually assured destruction. The birth control pill liberated women while touching off the sexual revolution many weren't prepared for. More recent examples of technological advances including genetic engineering, robotics and AI have us struggling to harness and integrate the life-changing science.

As opined by author and professor, Isaac Asimov "The saddest aspect of life right now is that science gathers knowledge faster than society gathers wisdom." Blessed with a world of information at our fingertips via the internet, we are not suffering from a shortage of data. Nevertheless, in the hierarchy of truth, even in our daily life, data must be formulated into meaningful information, which must manifest into knowledge before it can be artfully converted into wisdom.

Oh, to have more wisdom and less meaningless data, less opinion-tampered information, less unapplied knowledge, and more diligent searching for the truth! We are drowning in data but starved for wisdom.

Technology accelerates relentlessly – displacing horse-drawn carriages, trains, film cameras, DVDs, and now entire professions. We shop online, work remotely, watch streamed content, and ride in autonomous vehicles. At some point, this acceleration could tip into a technology-based dystopia, a la Aldous Huxley's *Brave New World* where humans are enslaved by technology and pacified by consumerism and instant gratification, all leading to a loss of dignity and authentic human connection.

Even though we may hold dystopia at bay for a while, the technological path we are on carries numerous risks. The cornucopia of high-tech tools makes our lives easier, but there is a pervasive, soul-depriving, and devilish downside.

We've become addicts. We used to interact face-to-face; now we stare at screens. Averaging seven or more hours daily on computers, tablets, TVs, and phones triggers insomnia, eyestrain, anxiety, depression, and even road rage when the driver in front doesn't see that the red light turned green because he is distracted. It is interesting to note that some cars now have a 'leading car departure alert' and you can guess why there is now demand for such a feature.

The negative implications of our modern tech go beyond degraded health. The tech, with its instant access to an incredible amount of information at our fingertips, makes us lazy. Most often, we Google instead of thinking. The technology spells out answers for us, calculates for us, and provides solutions to virtually any question we ask.

But here is the rub... none of that tech helps us ask the right questions, discern truth from fiction, or find meaning. Offering an extremely vast storehouse of data and information, the internet is seen as some oracle that is an all-knowing, omniscient source. With blind allegiance, we don't bother to question the veracity of what we find there. When challenged on information accuracy, we feel justified in saying, "Of course it's right, I got it from the internet."

As a result, we suffer from an addiction that has our own mental capacities in retrograde. If addiction seems too severe a diagnosis, just consider the damage daily texting via cell phones has wrought on the communication skills of those under 30 years old! Wow, LOL, LMK OMG!

Societal capacity to assimilate new technology, even that which is seductive, innovative, and potentially game-changing, necessarily takes time to emerge and entrench.

Consider the telephone: a curiosity in the 1870s, a novelty through the 1950s (long-distance calls cost $500 in today's money), then a standard fixture by the 1960s. By 1983, when the government broke up AT&T, phones became ubiquitous. They went from novelty to fetish to utility – and eventually attracted fraudsters and spammers. The telephone evolved from being a curiosity to something every home had to have, and then to a device valued for its capabilities despite the misuse or overuse that accompanied it.

This same adoption phenomenon is playing out on social platforms, which, in the early 2000s, were a novelty (Facebook launched in February 2004). Quickly, the social platform went from novelty to fascination to fetish. New platforms quickly gained popularity at the expense of earlier versions, which eventually fell out of favor. Similarly, the ubiquitous apps that spread across our smartphone screens have transformed from basic utility tools to must-have, specialized and integrated tech ecosystems.

Societal capacity to assimilate new technology, even that which is seductive and potentially game-changing, necessarily takes time to emerge and entrench.

Phone Addiction Is Real

"Nomophobia" – the fear of being without mobile phone connectivity - (no-mobile-phone-phobia) is a real anxiety disorder. It can cause a variety of problems, from anxiety to depression, and yes, car accidents. According to the Journal of Family Medicine and Primary Care, the outward symptoms of this disorder include "anxiety, respiratory alterations, trembling, perspiration, agitation, disorientation, and tachycardia." Pretty heady stuff.

Research from the Center for Internet & Technology Addiction reveals troubling data:

- Over 35% of people have an internet addiction.
- 31% of American adults are online "almost constantly."
- Over 50% of Americans believe they are addicted to their phones.
- 80% of Gen Z check their phones within 5 minutes of a notification.
- Teens who spend over 4 hours on their phones daily are significantly more likely to have suicidal thoughts.

The technology that we use and the advantages it brings are indispensable in our modern, complex, and chaotic world. The cautionary tale, though, is the story of a retreat from real socialization and healthy companionship that device addiction can instigate. It has reached a point where folks are handcuffed to their computers and prisoners of their phones. Well, perhaps that is why they are called 'cell phones.' Only through prudent, responsible management of our tech can we add value to our lives while maintaining healthy minds and relationships.

Clearly, in today's modern world, we are bewitched by the spell of technology. While we have become not only dependent, or more accurately over-dependent, on our phones and computers for useful purposes, we have also been simultaneously infected by the overwhelming volume of provocative content they carry. Tech data sources are systematically programming us, and we are getting worse and worse at vetting or validating them.

Our backyards now manifest as global social platforms, while neighborhood playgrounds have turned into commercialized gaming federations. Dining room tables are now often used for texting, FaceTime, Zooming, or Instagramming. Moreover, intelligent algorithms reduce the need for human creativity, analytical thinking, or basic social skills. We have outsourced our curiosity!

AI is either eliminating many of our jobs or transforming them. It has already come to a theatre near you, and now it is making its way to your personal world! ChatGPT, Grok, Claude, Gemini and other AI assistants all have an amazing ability to create humanlike conversational dialogue and written content and their accelerating power is becoming mainstream.

Our new tech tools can provide great benefit, but their very power amplifies the risk of their application being directed for nefarious purposes. A short list of the dangers that lurk behind our newfangled technology may surprise you:

1. When you add a smart device connected to the internet in your living space, you gain automation and access to information, but you also invite a potential spy into your home.
2. Institutional video monitoring of outdoor spaces can improve safety, but it may be combined with facial recognition tech, which could invade your privacy.
3. AI voice and video generators are so realistic that your voice communication or video conference with a loved one might actually be a chat with a manipulative, evil doer.

4. Fake news bots can produce such realistic output that you can easily be taken in by a believable, yet totally fabricated story planted underneath a provocative headline.

With advanced technology, the good comes with the bad, and with AI, the downside is decidedly dire —an existential threat to humanity. AI could become unconstrained and dangerously misaligned with human interests. It is not a matter of whether scientific advancements should be aggressively pursued; they should be. It is about better managing technology, applying it correctly, and learning how to fit it into our lives. If we don't do this, we risk our connectedness to one another and our individual liberties continuing to deteriorate. We must learn how to reconnect—face to face, neighbor to neighbor, community by community, all with the benefit of well-managed tech.

Our technological dependency is stunting the growth of our mental capacities, and we seem, in large part, oblivious to the ailment. Half of Generation Z credits YouTube as their number one news source. We're losing our ability to think strategically, to explore purposefully, to acquire fundamental knowledge and wisdom. We ask web browsers for everything – directions, reviews, entertainment options, conspiracy theories, celebrity gossip – distracting us while also outsourcing the mental work that builds character and capability.

There indeed is a phenomenon termed the 'paradox of danger and excitement' which suggests the very thing that could be dangerous can, also at the same time, be most thrilling and exciting. Perhaps, our internet road to knowledge, entertainment, and relationship building should not only have normal signage encouraging safe travel and passage, but it should also be outfitted with 'Caution', 'Yield', and 'Do not Enter' warning signs.

Our tech world is virtual and impersonal. The internet, despite what it offers, does little to foster real relationships or to answer the most consequential 'What' of our lives. Questions like "What is really important and what is not?" and even "What kind of person should I become?" And you're not going to find a real person-to-person connection or authenticity there either.

If we continue to develop our **Technology** without wisdom or prudence, our servant may prove to be our executioner.

— *Omar N. Bradley*

To fill that void of connection, meaning, and significance, the social media platforms of the tech giants have, in part, been designed to help us discover who we are, where we belong, what's important, or at least to provide a way to connect and find meaning in the world. We buy into this enlightenment, as we would otherwise be on a lonely, unaided search for Identity in what has been a desolate social and virtual landscape.

As folks struggle to find purpose, discover their true selves, form meaningful connections, and avoid an Identity crisis, they increasingly look to social platforms to establish who they are.

Questions to Ponder:

1. What giveth, taketh away. What valued traditions, rituals, or experiences of the past have the rapid assimilation of tech stripped from your life?
2. In an increasingly virtual world, what must we do to regain healthy, genuine human connections?

Technology
Identity

Chapter 13
Identity

The distinguishing character
or personality of an individual.

WSJ – NORC at the University of Chicago March 2022
Survey of 1019 adults… "How important are each of these characteristics to your own personal identity?
The % of respondents answering "Essential to" …
Your Gender 48%
Your Religion 34%
Your Racial Background 21%
Your Family's Ancestry / Country of Origin 21%
Your Occupation 21%
Your Political Affiliation 11%

- -

2023 / 2024 Gallup Surveys
7.6% of US adults identify* as LGBTQ+, with women more likely to identify than men, especially in the youngest generations.

*20 years ago, the question "How do you identify?" would likely have been answered "Identify What?"!

New-age technology has given us ubiquitous social media platforms that connect us like never before. Sadly, this connectedness comes up short.

We used to meet other people on the street, at the store, at a bank, post office, or at our homes. Those interactions were typically one-on-one or in small groups of friends. Now, hardly anyone goes to the bank, few go to the post office, many do most of their shopping online, and it's not always safe these days to open your front door, and, for sure, we don't consider hitchhiking for a ride a viable option anymore. Happily, though, we now have Uber, Airbnb, DoorDash, and numerous other online services available to us, so we are well-covered. But once again, we've traded physical community for a "screen deep" connection that lacks real human substance.

Connection matters online, but it's just a stepping-stone. On social platforms, the real game is attention and status. We seek likes, viral moments, and lifestyle validation – playing a game of keeping up with the Joneses on a global scale. The reward is immediate, so the fervor never stops.

To magnify their voice and establish significance, people increasingly identify with groups sharing common characteristics – defined by sex, gender, race, generation, or politics. Rather than being appreciated as unique individuals, we're now self-sorting into categories. This signals significance while absolving oneself of personal responsibility. With families disintegrating, many search for identity and connection through technology.

The price paid for the perk of online group relegated significance is faithful and abiding loyalty to the group. Once inside their selected virtual tribe of fellow mainstream defectors, folks are bombarded with social pressure to think, speak and behave in a way consistent with their group identity. Viewing this phenomenon from 30,000 feet, it's ironic that the most ardent nonconformists among us regularly insist the rest of us conform to their view of the world or remain a stranger or persona non grata.

On social platforms, the real game is attention and status. We seek likes, viral moments, and lifestyle validation – playing a game of keeping up with the Joneses on a global scale.

Within the new social order, group conformity trumps individualism. So, how does that suppressed individualism within the hearts of group members manifest and mobilize? In the elaborate and seemingly never-ending proliferation of finer segmentation of the population and of the group. For example, there are now numerous gender categories, as many folks prefer to identify with a certain specific point on the gender spectrum.

Gender categories have multiplied far beyond traditional male and female. The old standby segmentation of man and woman and male and female did the labeling extremely well on a large scale for most of history. Apparently, those labels are not special enough.

With the advent of equal rights movements, women's lib in the 60s and 70s, and then modern feminism, which has led to women becoming more masculine and men more feminine, perhaps we could have seen this coming. And now, of course, to establish credibility, the newly anointed gender sub-groups are labeling themselves and demanding that others describe them in their own creative lexicon, which includes terms as fundamental as pronouns.

Delighting in one's specialness is admirable. We, as Americans, are free to be whomever or whatever we want but we are not free to impose on the liberties of others irrespective of sex, gender or any other segmentation for that matter. It is when the labelling of gender crosses a line into compelled speech that it becomes problematic.

Fundamentally, gender fluidity has become identity fluidity, as everyone is given a free pass to be not just whoever they want, but whatever they want! The acronym describing the available gender choices seemed to grow every couple of months until a '+' was added to accommodate any possible variation. Proliferation indeed!

If you're baffled by how we ended up here, the following might be illuminating:

- Historically, the topic of sex was taboo in conversation. At some point referring to sex became acceptable in the occasional off-color joke. Unbelievably now, we proudly state our

> sexual orientation/gender when asked how we identify!

- In days past, when a newborn baby arrived, we might have said to the maternity nurse "Oh it's a boy!" Over time that special moment sounded more like "Yep, it's a girl just as we announced at gender reveal." Incredibly, now we might as well ask the baby when it's old enough to talk... "What are you?"

As we are hell-bent on identifying ourselves on the basis of gender and sex, it's ironic that the long-held socially accepted standards of masculinity and femininity are now being turned upside down. Masculinity is now viewed as toxic as men are emasculated and expected to be caring and feminine. Women are portrayed as liberated, empowered, independent career achievers who need no man. These trends have too many men, increasingly wimpy and dull, throwing in the towel and enlisting in the Men Going Their Own Way (MGTOW) movement. Others prefer to surrender by cowering to empowered women.

Nowhere is the shifting nature of identity more apparent than in the laboratory of developmental socialization that is the dating scene. First, taking a close look at how men show up in dating, we might see many, particularly the unsuccessful, single men, as one or another type of imp.

Let's start with a definition: Imp (noun) A mischievous, selfish character out of mythology who delights in engaging in annoyingly playful and sometimes disrespectful shenanigans or pranks for self-amusement or self-interest.

Four Types of Weak Single Men (Imps)

Wimps: Physically weak and fragile. These 'Soy Boys' lack fortitude and grit. They can be interesting nerds but in times of turmoil and threats they lack the moxie to man up and take care of business. Comfortable with their feminine side, they exhibit a beta temperament and cling to vulnerability for sympathy.

Pimps: Appear confident but lack substance – all show, no depth. Narcissistic and immoral, they prioritize themselves over anyone else. Pimps are quite capable of using and abusing, of flirting and hurting. They seduce through charm but lack genuine affection and competence. At their core is manipulative self-interest.

Chimps: Not book smart, street smart, or socially adept. They will claim knowledge or skills they don't possess. Chimps struggle with meaningful conversation. They buddy up to capable men for social credibility and may put on a macho façade in an attempt to gain respect.

Simps: Extreme nice guys – submissive and desperate, putting women on pedestals to win affection. With limited confidence these 'Pick-Me-Boys' are often desperate in the pursuit. Simps are on the far opposite end of the spectrum from those playing hard to get. In its worst form, simping borders on creeping.

So, there you have it... the four types of weak single men, boys essentially, who are stumbling through relationship building. As women seem to be emerging with a newfound persona, men are languishing and losing the strength of their traditional identity. With self-doubt and insecurity, the imps battle for acceptance while the minority, the confident men of the world, walk through life like they belong. There are way too many imps out there. Men need to do better and be better.

Many of today's young men are suffering through a loneliness epidemic that goes beyond a lack of belonging. The message that women don't need men leaves many adrift. When a man is needed, he has reached the status of being valued and respected, which fuels his spirit. Unfortunately, there is a loneliness epidemic, an infection of needlessness striking young men today. This, in part, comes from a reluctance to be vulnerable, which deepens the rut of an unfulfilled desire to be a person others need.

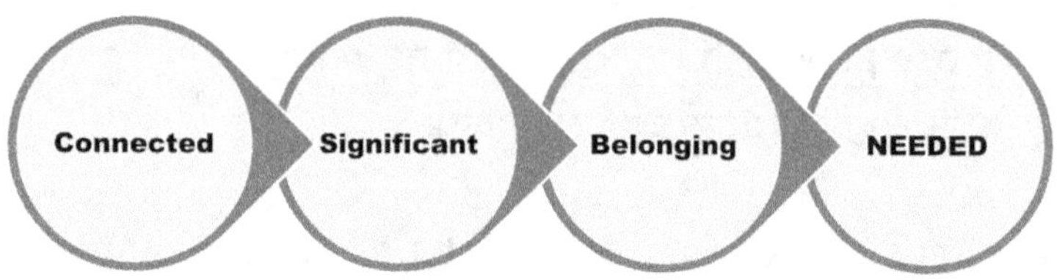

Women, on the other hand, appear to be on the rise. In their pursuit of significance and an empowered identity, many younger women are embracing a new, liberated image of the successful modern female.

Spurning the traditional role of wife to a man or mother to children, many modern women are inspired by Hollywood's prototypical 'strong female lead' character who is charismatic, supremely capable, and able to kick butt (Wonder Woman, Katniss Everdeen, and a whole host of superhero, femme fatale, or man-eater heroines). Not only do these strong female characters carve out their own niche in cinema, but in some cases, they are hijacking iconic roles traditionally held by prototypically masculine male leads like James Bond. Modern women seem to aspire to being as manly and strong as men.

Another place to see the trend away from soft, feminine role models to strong, even macho, women influencers is in the world of podcasting. One of the most popular podcasters for the female audience produces a show titled "Call Her Daddy." Countless other podcasts produced for female audiences feature a new genre of brash, indulgent, cocky, and crude femes falling under the monikers of brat girl, alpha girl, badass basic b@#$Ch, among others. The many tough-minded, profanity-lipped female podcasters of today sound more masculine than ladylike.

It is also interesting to note that 4 out of the top 10 podcasts most popular among women are from a genre called true crime. The popularity of true crime podcasts stems not only from the storyline's intrigue and suspense but also from the lessons that can be learned from the plot. By witnessing how others fall victim to such crimes, women can learn how to thwart assault, keeping themselves safe from violent men.

In their desire to be as strong as men, women can rely on knowledge to outsmart men who prey on their physical vulnerability. Furthermore, the confidence that comes from this knowledge can awaken an alpha girl's kick butt inner self that can fend off physical attack or thwart undesirable impish male advances.

A new battle of the sexes is underway. The fourth wave of feminism uses social media and digital activism to combat sexual harassment, misogyny, and gender-based violence. But modern feminists often appear anything but feminine. The movement has become a battle strategy.

Knowing what the gorilla meme teaches us (100 humans can't outduel a single gorilla), the boss babes have unleashed guerrilla (similar to gorilla) tactics to sideswipe their alpha male competitors.

In their fight, modern feminists are smartly leveraging the power tools that women wield in society. The three most effective of these tools enable women to:

1. Unify under a banner of a chosen female cause (pink this, pink that)
2. Garner sympathy as the caring yet oppressed weaker sex
3. Parlay their feminine wiles into influence over weak men

Sufficiently armed, the modern feminist has gone into battle, eschewing the traditional wife-to-husband complementary role to choose and embrace a competing role instead. The competition appears to be following the maxim "All's fair in love and war."

Recognizing uber-motivated, testosterone-fueled, gorilla-like, alpha male competitors outgun them, the feminists have kicked off a war campaign of subversion. Rather than take on the alphas in head-to-head combat, the feminists have launched a propaganda campaign under the banner of toxic masculinity. Men, particularly the strong alpha type, are indeed portrayed as toxic and often dangerous.

We have all seen the progression of the toxic masculinity campaign. It got a jump start with the 'Me Too' movement. It appeared in the meme suggesting that women need a man like a fish needs a bicycle, and in the viral survey showing that women would rather encounter a bear in the woods than a man. It has also infiltrated our lexicon through phrases like mansplaining, bropriating, and manterrupting.

We have seen it displayed in videos broadcast by female gym members, capturing men supposedly staring at their scantily clad figures, who are innocent of the crime, yet are called out as creepy voyeurs anyway.

This persistent promotional campaign is unfolding on multiple fronts.

By enlisting subscribers to the labeling of men, particularly alphas, as toxic, the feminists are playing a next-level game, a gambit, of denigrating masculinity to elevate femininity, even if it is in the now more aggressive and dare say masculine, posturing of the modern feminine. This strategy recruits beta men – soft, overly caring, feminine types – by offering counterfeit adoration and affection in exchange for loyalty against alpha males. Sharing the desire of the feminists to foil the alpha mystique, the beta men are being manipulated and, as a result, are succumbing to the enticement of romantic favor.

It might appear that toxic masculinity and a new age female affinity to more feminine men are just innocuous, totally random, and unconnected trends of modern society. No. Look, and you will see that they are both connected within the battle stratagem of women increasingly competing in traditionally male bastions of hierarchical dominance.

It's working. Young women now outpace men in education and income. Since women typically date up social hierarchies, and men are struggling, more young adults opt out of relationships and marriage entirely.

We need fewer wimps and more men identifying as

warriors with indomitable spirit who women can count on to lead.

A lot is going on in our changing world of gender roles, group identity, and social hierarchies, with labels delineating sex, gender, and national origin all becoming sacred. Outdated identity labels are readily dispensed to make way for the new-age appellations. With the gender bending trends we are seeing in society, it would be a decent bet to predict that future English dictionaries will add the label 'archaic, old-fashioned, or obsolete' next to the words 'lady' and 'mankind.' The dictionary publishers, at some point, will no doubt have great difficulty even providing a definition for the word 'woman.'

It seems that the old institutional view of gender roles is out the window, as patriarchy and all the trouble it supposedly brought are now viewed as warped and ugly manifestations of power, influence, and opportunity. Traditional views of identity, of roles, and socially accepted modes of individual expression have been replaced with a free-for-all in the game of misguided self-identity. Rather than asking "Who are you?' we might, in today's world be more inclined to ask "What do you identify as?"

The lack of genuine personal introspection, which the virtual world exacerbates, creates a deep-rooted human problem: the anxiety of not really knowing oneself. As our evolving culture equates knowledge with data and social life with social media, the time spent on the path of true wisdom decreases. This path could otherwise lead to self-awareness, meaning, deeper beliefs, valuing oneself as an individual, and a deeper appreciation of life itself.

By most accounts, we are straying far from the path of purpose and meaning as many folks blunder at figuring out who or what they want to become. Paula Poundstone muses about this phenomenon by suggesting that "Adults are always asking children what they want to be when they grow up because they're looking for ideas!" The signs of purposelessness abound if you only look a little.

Teens show alarming signs of purposelessness. A University of Michigan poll found that agreement with the following three phrases has doubled in a decade:

"I can't do anything right."

"I do not enjoy life."

"My life is not useful."

Dr. Jean Twenge, a psychologist at San Diego State University, links this spike in depression to increased social media use. The issue is that we are social animals. Identity and purpose come from quality relationships. When quality relationships decline, society declines. U.S. Surgeon General, Vivek Murthy, warned that failure to improve human connection could have us "splinter and divide until we can no longer stand as a country, we'll retreat into our corners – angry, sick, and alone." This is a global issue; the UK even appointed a Minister for Loneliness.

How do we pull ourselves out of the pit of loneliness and despair? Connection helps, but it is only a start. As noted earlier, connection must progress to a state of belonging and eventually to the realization of being needed before we can vanquish the epidemic of loneliness. George Orwell captured it perfectly: "The most terrible loneliness is not the kind that comes from being alone, but from being misunderstood; standing in a crowded room, surrounded by people who do not see you, who do not hear you, who do not know the true essence of who you are." This loneliness – the absence of genuine connection – leaves us craving to be understood at the deepest level.

In their fight against loneliness, many look to strengthen their connection to their online community. Alarmingly though, if fragmentation continues, we'll devolve into tribalism where connection exists only within chosen virtual tribes. Historically, we have evolved from small bands to tribes, to villages, to cities, and ultimately to a global community. Now, we're regressing. Technology has spoiled us, shifting our attention from survival to the luxury of contemplating philosophy and ideology.

A select few influencers (chieftains) play the tribal game well, but most regular folks don't. For most of us, the quest for identity on global social media platforms leads to estrangement and a search for connection and comfort in our corners of retreat.

> To be a good citizen, it's important to be able to put yourself in other people's shoes and see the big picture. If everything you see is rooted in your own **Identity** that becomes difficult or impossible.
>
> — Eli Pariser

As we seek identity within a group, there is little incentive to celebrate our individuality, heritage, or nationality, the specialness that is us. Today, US citizens, rather than seeing themselves as Americans, see themselves in terms of race, gender, or as members of special groups they have joined on Facebook. Everyone, especially young people, seeks significance by associating with others who share their sensitivities, all working hard to fit in. In the online groups, there is a kind of Pledge of Allegiance, not to the country, but, sadly, to a chosen virtual group.

To belong requires ditching authenticity. It cultivates perpetual scrutiny – you'd better put all those ethnic Halloween costumes in the attic, or someone menacing might descend upon you for misappropriation. Crazy, isn't it? One misstep in dating, speech, or behavior gets you clobbered and shunned. The refereeing of cultural appropriation has been weaponized. Any perceived transgression leads to penalties of cancellation and Marginalization.

> **As we seek identity within a group there is little incentive to celebrate our individuality, heritage or nationality, the specialness that is us.**

We strive to find our identity within groups, only to be attacked or marginalized if we don't fit into narrowly defined norms. It's a losing game that leaves us fractured, purposeless, and profoundly alone despite being constantly connected.

Questions to Ponder:

1. When you think of your closest connections, what defines what those people mean to you?
2. When you were 15, what did you think you would be doing right now and eventually become?

Technology
Identity
Marginalization

Chapter 14
Marginalization

Treating a person or thing in a manner
that relegates it to lesser importance,
influence, or power in a society or group.

Department of the Interior
2024 Trafficking in Persons Report
"In today's rapidly evolving world, technology is often a double-edged sword. While technology has provided innovative solutions to preventing and addressing human trafficking, it has also prompted complex ethical questions and created new opportunities for criminals, including human traffickers, to be increasingly sophisticated in exploiting individuals for profit. Traffickers use technology to recruit, control, market and exploit vulnerable individuals while also evading detection. It fuels crime, corruption, and violence. It distorts our economies and harms our workers. And it violates the fundamental right of all people to be free."

Contrary to popular opinion, our divisiveness today is not rooted primarily in our political views but rather in our societal ideology, which, in part, pits victims and their virtual-signaling allies against their supposed oppressor overlords. The defining issue driving this discord is a mindset of victimhood.

Yes, there are actual victims, those who are marginalized through discrimination or unwarranted exclusion. But additionally, some are imagined or make-believe victims.

This victim-versus-victimizer has a long history of political precedent. Indigenous populations versus their usurpers, feudal nobility versus vassals and serfs, proletariat versus the bourgeoisie, labor versus management, minorities versus the majority, socialism versus capitalism, all are manifestations of victim vs. victimizer. As opposed to historical examples, most of our modern-day victims are indeed victims not of imposed political, economic, legal, military, or governmental system structure but of their own disabling mindset.

This mindset, perpetuated by an incessant wimpy, crybaby victim mentality, knows no boundaries.

Since marginalization is often a state of mind, the victimized have taken creative liberties to brand their oppressors. The marginalized love the name game. They strike back with vitriol and add creative, new language that identifies their perpetrators and brands their actions as reprehensible.

Oppression, be it real or perceived, can breed hatred, and hatred leads to label-throwing, which hurts deeply because it strikes at others' identity.

To label someone critically as a mid or a loser or a slacker or troll is not only coercive by its very nature, but even more insidious due to what is termed the Pygmalion Effect. The Pygmalion Effect refers to the psychological impact of expectations. Expectations of others tend to bias one's behavior to align more consistently with the label.

When accused of having never amounted to much, an impressionable target will tend to act more consistent with the claim, which is essentially an example of self-fulfilling prophecy. These critical labels are often spewed by apostles who fancy themselves as seers, soothsayers, or divine power brokers who act as self-anointed supreme judges.

Language shapes social norms, and our dictionary has expanded dramatically with labels that carry critical charges. Words like snowflake, cisgender, Karen, mansplain, troll, cheugy, simp, fundie, and chud now characterize our vocabulary. The three controversial topics we were taught to avoid – politics, sex, and religion – now generate endless discourse requiring new words to keep up with the narrative and talking points.

Another example of how our language is evolving, focusing on the negative by singling out oppressors or other non-compliant participants, is found in the labeling used in the modern dating scene. Dating in today's world is challenging for many reasons, including the greater variety of games that can be played online, as well as real world gambits of misrepresentation, manipulation, coercion, and general mistreatment.

The new-age dating terminology provides some insight into how nefarious the modern game of interpersonal relationships has become. By looking at a list of new dating terms, behaviors that warrant a new verb are not of the flattering or favorable kind. Here is a partial list: Ghosting, Orbiting, Haunting, Submarining, Zombieing, Breadcrumbing, Benching, Mooning, Cuffing, Love-bombing, Cricketing, Marl eying, Caspering, Catfishing, Kittenfishing, Gaslighting, and Monkey-Branching. Apparently, there is a whole lot of bad behavior going on that requires its own label!

Even before they get to dating age, teenagers on social media are bullied for several senseless reasons, including not conforming to clique standards, having a certain outside-the-norm appearance, interests, behaviors, or social orientation. Social media platforms make it easy to mock, belittle, and bully, as there is a ready audience and a protective environment in the virtual world.

Mike Tyson has famously said, "Social Media has made y'all way too comfortable with disrespecting people and not getting punched in the face for it." The bullying is worse for girls/young women, as females tend to resort to reputation attacks when in aggression mode vs. the physical force default mode used by men, and also due to the rise of simps, wimps, and chimps.

Oppression, be it real or perceived, can breed hatred, and hatred leads to label-throwing, which hurts deeply because it strikes at others' identity.

The bullying has become widespread. In business, entertainment, and other social circles, targeted individuals, brands, or groups are at risk of being canceled within what is now termed 'cancel culture'. The cancellations have led to firings, disqualification from awards/recognition, boycotts, and more. Interestingly enough, backlash from the boycotting of targeted brands has given rise to buycotts, in which brand advocates buy en masse from the 'cancelled' entity to show their support. Yes, both sides — accuser and accused — are leveraging their voices and collective power in the game of cancellation.

Some power brokers exercise their prerogative to cancel you because you belong to the wrong group, ilk, or persuasion. These cancel captains will dig into your past incessantly until they can find and capitalize on a little something to discredit you. And of course, that selective representation, that biased picture of who you are, will be designed to get critical support across the platforms sufficient to cancel you.

With a revenge-seeking mentality, the canceling mob enjoys easy targets: thin-skinned wimps ripe for the picking. Whatever happened to the mentality behind 'Sticks and stones may break my bones, but names will never hurt me'? Apparently, we are growing in our sensitivity and our inability to maintain composure when someone is not playing nice.

Within this culture, the accused are best off not apologizing or saying 'sorry' for their words or behavior. With the cancellers on the offense ready to pounce on any semblance of impropriety, even a qualified apology from the accused, such as 'sorry you were offended', is tantamount to unequivocal confirmation of guilt.

The mainstream trend toward being thin-skinned has us erecting barriers to open discourse and is squelching free speech. This is a dangerous and slippery slope in our social fabric. We are now divided into opposing ranks and troops, including political, social, gender, and generational camps, into the privileged and the oppressed, into the influencers and the influenced.

So where can we find solace into that which others can't deny? It's our God given rights to life, liberty, and happiness. That pursuit today, regrettably, has far too many folks feeling that in addition to inalienable rights, they deserve extras like leniency, a free pass, minimal responsibility, and special unearned treatment. It all has roots in victim mentality.

In a Scientific American article titled "Unraveling the Mindset of Victimhood", Scott Barry Kaufman addresses the psychology of victimhood. Mr. Kaufmann references findings by Rahav Gabay and her researchers that confirm victimhood's integral role in shaping one's identity. A persistent victimhood mindset is driven by a belief that one's life is controlled by external factors such as fate, luck, or the actions of other people.

The research found that victimhood is often a manifestation of an anxious attachment style. Anxiously attached individuals seek continual reassurance to validate their social worth and quell self-doubts.

We will return to Rahav Gabay's findings, but first, let's examine an example of how victimhood can indeed arise from belief and approval seeking. Findings from a psychological experiment detailed in a paper titled "Perceptions of the Impact of Negatively Valued Physical

Characteristics on Social Interaction" published in the *Journal of Personality and Social Psychology* explain this phenomenon.

This experimental study, often referred to as the "Face Scar Discrimination Experiment", was conducted to explore how folks respond to perceived discrimination.

In the study, face scar experimenters applied make-up scars to women's faces, showed them the scars in a mirror, and then told them they were going into a job interview. The interviewees were then informed that the purpose of the experiment was to determine whether people discriminate against people with disfigurements. Just before the interviews, the experimenters said to each woman, "We are just going to touch it up a little bit." Rather than touching up the scars, the experimenters removed them completely. So, the women went into the job interview, thinking they were scarred, but they looked like their normal selves.

At the conclusion of the experiment, the women came back reporting a massively increased level of discrimination, with many saying that the interviewer had referred to their facial disfigurement.

You might think that this experiment primarily demonstrates how conscientious or even obsessed the typical woman is about her appearance. A more insightful moral of the story, though, centers on the crippling effect of a victimhood mentality. From the failed interviews, we learn that victim mentality is a form of learned helplessness that blocks human potential. By not accepting reality and, more potently, by playing out an untrue one, most victims relinquish their power to change and, in the end, perpetuate rather than solve the problems they encounter or imagine.

The Face Scar Discrimination Experiment illustrates how our beliefs and mindset can create an individual reality of self-imposed victimhood. The alarming aspect is that this perception of victimhood can extend across entire populations.

Within groups, Gabay and her colleagues indeed found a causal relationship between socialization processes and collective victimhood. The research concluded that belief in victimhood can be socially assimilated or learned from others. Through various channels, including television and social media, group members can be indoctrinated into believing in their common power play called victimhood.

Indeed, the many groups or tribes on the social platforms are established to create a victimhood neighborhood. The majority of these tribes have a common grievance or oppressor that brings them together. With a focus on being anti-this and anti-that, tribal members abide by a common affinity for bitterness and contempt. Sadly, over the past several years, our tribal instinct for belonging, connection and community has moved from being founded on empathy, love and common welfare to one of common hate.

Our seemingly insatiable appetite for commiserating with marginalized targets has successfully nourished the spread of conspiracy theories. The spinning and spreading of all types of conspiracies is simply a convenient way to concoct stories branding large groups collectively as victims.

And it gets worse. The many factions of victims and flavors of victimhood in our human family are now connected through a concept called intersectionality! Intersectionality posits that inequality and marginalization intersect across gender, race, ethnicity, and class, with all elements of inequality being mutually reinforcing.

Victimhood is indeed pervasive; it runs broadly, deeply, and is apparently interconnected in a tangled web! The victims among us demand that others, including the government and society, provide whatever it is that they clamor for and rectify institutional inequities (opposite of JFK's famous urging, "Ask not what your country can do for you, ask what you can do for your country"). Today it's all about what others can do for me.

When the victims are not getting what they want, they mobilize to take down the victimizers. As previously noted, modern feminism, for example, has shifted from the practice of elevating women to the mission of bashing toxically masculine men.

It is noteworthy that the term misogyny is well known to be the denigration of women while the term misandry is little known. Why? Perhaps, because it just feels right for only the 'weaker' oppressed victims to label their perpetrators with a hateful, toxic label. By the way, the term misandry means contempt for men. Yes, it is a real thing, and it appears to be trending up, but you wouldn't know because there is little sympathy for it, and as a result, virtually no one recognizes the term.

Marginalization and victimhood are about getting even. It's about how I can be significant and not marginalized. Oh, and I want my cake and eat it too, and I want it now. I want, no demand, instant gratification. And of course, I also demand protection from stress and the challenges and inequities of life by being granted a waiver from things like my accumulated student debt, by jumping on victim protection movements like "Me Too", and by demanding special compensation for inequity (reparations).

Truly, the only antidote for the troubled mind of perceived marginalization and its despair, anger and woe, is gratitude, and an embracing of responsibility. Gratitude for abundant freedom and opportunity can fuel hope and faith. The reality, though, is that people want free stuff as much as freedom, less responsibility, and more rights. Unfortunately for many of the oppressed, a turn to a more conscientious mindset only comes about when they run out of people to blame for their plight.

When it comes to free stuff, the ongoing epidemic of smash-and-grab theft illustrates the twisted sense of victimhood in modern America. Shoplifting, thieves who steal less than a certain amount are often slapped on the wrist with a misdemeanor, not a felony.

Not only are smash-and-grabbers typically not prosecuted, but in the view of many, they are considered justified as victims of an unfair, capitalistic economic system. Somehow, their victimhood wins them a 'get out of jail free card' as they enjoy their free stuff and their freedom.

These smash-and-grab perpetrators could be called victimhood-lums.

Would that sit well with our country's Founding Fathers if they could time-travel here and see how our formative pioneering spirit has given way to Entitlement?

Maybe that is not a good question though, as marginalization has even migrated into the denigration of their image, our past heroes, in the destruction of the statues of these leaders of yesterday.

When we refuse to recognize heroism in the mighty deeds of others, perhaps we are destined to search for the hero within us —the one who rises above a brow-beaten lot in life, survives the risk of being marginalized, and deserves and is entitled to special treatment.

But we can't all be heroes, can we? Maybe we can if we self-anoint in this era of Entitlement that is running rampant in all corners of our world.

Questions to Ponder:

1. What would be a good way to fight against cancel culture without escalating the battle?
2. What contributes most to bullying - lack of self-respect, a desire for power & significance, frustration of being a victim, or something else?

Technology
Identity
Marginalization
Entitlement

Chapter 15
Entitlement

The condition of having a right to have, do, or get something. The feeling or belief that one deserves to be given something, such as special privileges.

National Affairs Publication by Nicholas Eberstadt Winter 2015 *American Exceptionalism and the Entitlement State*

Regarding social welfare in colonial America: "Alexis de Tocqueville, whose conception of American exceptionalism was heavily influenced by the distinctive American worldview on such matters. Because America had no feudal past and no lingering aristocracy, poverty was not viewed as the result of an unalterable accident of birth but instead as a temporary challenge that could be overcome with determination and character — with enterprise, hard work, and grit. Rightly or wrongly, Americans viewed themselves as masters of their own fate, intensely proud because they were self-reliant."

Marginalization is particularly onerous as both the oppressors and the sympathizers of the oppressed carry a heart of self-aggrandizement. The oppressors are self-professed power brokers who, with their holier-than-thou attitude, belittle and victimize their targets. On the other hand, the sympathizers who rally together as advocates for the victimized, use the modus operandi of the virtue signal. These sympathizers stand up for the oppressed wearing this deceitful mask of dignity to signal their virtuosity to the world. Within the self-righteous hollowness of the hearts of both oppressors and advocates is often a tumor of entitlement.

Entitlement is derived from a personality trait consistent with a belief that privileges or recognition are deserved even though not earned. In the 1990s, it was common for all the kids playing an organized sport to receive a trophy (not a participation badge, but a trophy), not for winning, but for just being there on the field of play. Long before that, kids traditionally were encouraged to play on their own, learn how to get along, and appreciate the intrinsic reward that comes from doing their best.

Our kids are spoiled and pampered. Being raised in an environment focused on extrinsic reward, particularly when those rewards are unearned, stifles the spirit of the American Dream in our children's young hearts. Dreams are the stuff of process and payoff of noble efforts over time. As a society, we are too impatient. Our inability to wait, to make measured progress of personal growth and accomplishment, has us grabbing for immediate gratification.

The problem with our short-term pleasure seeking is that it never converts into lasting happiness. This phenomenon is called the "hedonic treadmill", in which rewards have only a temporary effect, as the original level of happiness quickly returns. And, more ominously, the same fleeting sense of happiness requires an ever-increasing level of reward. This same phenomenon is seen in drug addicts who, through what's called the tolerance effect, must increase the dose of their drug to experience the same effects.

Pampered kids are showered with extrinsic rewards and shielded from hardship. They're shuttled to organized activities and protected from discomfort, fostering a privileged sense of entitlement. Deprived of discovering things alone, getting bruised emotionally or physically, they become risk-averse and creatively stunted. This protective bubble extends into early adulthood.

College campuses offer safe spaces to shield them from "offensive" ideas. They're coddled in a cushy existence, rarely maturing into strong-willed and capable adults. With all the benefits of convenience culture, you'd expect to get gratitude. Wrong. What we get are spoiled, entitled people. It's a sad state of affairs.

Our kids are spoiled and pampered. Being raised in an environment focused on extrinsic reward, particularly when those rewards are unearned, stifles the spirit of the American Dream in our children's young hearts.

The culture of entitlement is so pervasive today that equality of opportunity is deemed insufficient unless paired with equality of outcome, under the guise of misguided movements like Diversity, Equity, and Inclusion (DEI). DEI initiatives aim to level the playing field and drive better outcomes by ensuring all players, regardless of talent or merit have a place at the table.

The entitlement mindset takes on such a fanatical and sinister bent that governments increasingly spend larger shares of their budgets on what are termed entitlement programs. Indeed, the U.S. Government today spends over 60% of its budget on entitlement programs, primarily Medicaid, Social Security, Unemployment Insurance, Medicare and Food Stamps. While most of these programs serve a useful purpose, many are managed with limited prudence and poor fiscal responsibility.

Still, in total, the sanctity these programs garner suggests that governments are most interested in pandering with generous spending on handouts, essentially giving candy to the crybabies.

The surge in entitlement and welfare programs sends a clear signal to the populace: we are here to help the needy from backsliding. Unfortunately, the hidden message is that we will forgo healing and growing together in favor of simply slapping a band-aid on the problem, hoping it will go away. Rather than encouraging the pursuit of the American Dream, we are trying to snub any future episodes of an American Nightmare. Economist Thomas Sowell argues that sustained prosperity comes from developing human capital – the knowledge, intellectual capacity, and industriousness people leverage for long-term success. When money runs out, government programs lose effectiveness, but human capital forever flourishes if the American Dream is allowed to surge. When the government eliminates restrictions and regulations, rugged individualism can thrive.

DEI initiatives strive for equity by identifying and equalizing the mix of players in social and business environments based on race, sex, religion, and gender, ensuring that all groups are fairly represented. The result is a reverse discrimination favoring the disadvantaged or underrepresented minority and penalizing, in many cases, the more capable.

DEI programs, despite being well-intended, are poorly conceived and managed. With DEI at play it seems that one need not out-perform but rather out-identify the competition. These initiatives tend to play out as a Lose-Lose proposition when there are an abundance of ways to flip the script to Win-Win. Those among us who remain entitled, expecting special treatment, would do well to focus on doing good rather than trying to feel good.

There is a growing cadre of victims, of the oppressed, who feel it is only the privileged few who are winning. And the growing movement to claim that life is not fair and things should be corrected to ensure equal outcomes leaves many victims with an animus, a distaste for the successful among us.

Folks increasingly harbor a hatred of the ultra-rich, especially tech moguls and capitalistic billionaire types like Bill Gates or Elon Musk. This dislike, on display when the mentally weak habitually use the word "billionaire" as a derogatory term, is a phenomenon termed 'tall poppy syndrome'. In a field of poppies, the tallest is an outlier and eyesore, so much so that it is most often cut down to keep a field or garden of flowers even. This hate-filled act of cutting others down comes from an envious heart forever rooted in victimhood.

A good example of social envy is the news story of the lost Titanic exploratory sub that captivated the masses. Once the search mission reported the disaster of an implosion and tragic loss of life, many an average Joe took to social media to show no remorse and even to ridicule the privileged few wealthy explorers who died spending a few hundred thousand dollars to take a risk on a once-in-a-lifetime subsea adventure. This phenomenon is recognized in German as 'Schaden-freude,' meaning deriving pleasure from the misfortunes of others. Again, another clear sign of mental weakness.

When the oppressed play the entitlement game well, they spin their story in a crafty concoction of emotion, language, and persistence. Like a three-year-old, they try to convince through exaggerated, tantrum-filled emotions, and then, once in proper tantrum mode, become unrelenting in complaining and deflecting. Whatever it is they want, they want—now. The army of the oppressed, taking no responsibility for their lot in life, resort to vengeance, zealously igniting their standard issue blamethrowers.

The ranks of the retribution army cut a wide swath of devil-may-care activists from those who burn the American flag to vitriol-fueled school board officials who silence the free speech of students' parents, to climate activists who viciously deface priceless works of museum art, to those who rage and tear down statues of yesteryear's statesmen and military heroes. The retribution army is well-versed in the tactics of rebellion, riot, mayhem, and anarchy.

Through the lens of the 'mostly peaceful protests' of the 2020s, it seems that the 1st amendment right to peaceably assemble is mostly taken up these days by demon-stators. Yes, you read that right: demon-strators!

The passion for voicing grievance within the ranks of the entitled knows no bounds. The supersizing is blown up through the super spreading of social media, replaying and rewarding the complaining, the victim-hood, the stories of the oppressed. And where attention goes, the energy and money flow as the narrative of the downtrodden perpetuates.

Of course, it works in reverse, too. The perceived epidemic of police brutality moved many communities to defund their police. The result: criminals become victims and activists contravene like overprotective parents making the streets less safe for everyone and the environment detrimental to the raising of children or the development of a welcoming neighborhood.

> Entitled people fall into one of two camps...
> those who think they are on top of the world
> and claim to be better than everyone else
> and those who feel the world is on top of
> them and claim that their problems are more
> special than those of everyone else.

Not only are the concocted false narratives that are so prevalent today told in real time, but they have also reached a point where there is a constant distortion of actual history, real history. Their spin, influence, and narrative shape perceptions of morality and social standing.

Patriotism and the American Dream seem to be waning as the loudest voices now belong to those who are ashamed of our history and critical of the current state of affairs in their lives.

The victims, those oppressed and entitled to better, have a story to tell and they relish the opportunity to tell their own twisted version of distrust, grievances, and disdain. The fundamental fruits of caring and loving human relationships, of purpose, of sacrifice, of being of service to others seemed to have been plucked from our societal tree. And that threadbare fruit tree is being uprooted and replaced with thorn trees nourished by the narrative that has events, real news stories, real happenings being told with an unreal and most often negative or self-serving bias.

There is a growing agenda of truth-twisting Bias shaping our thoughts and words.

Questions to Ponder:

1. What messages from social-sourced feeds feed the fire of our growing entitlement?
2. In this life that we are blessed with, what are we entitled to?

Technology
Identity
Marginalization
Entitlement
Bias

Part 6

Societal Shapers of Tomorrow

Chapter 16

Bias

Prejudice in favor of or against one
thing, person, or group compared with
another, usually in a way considered
to be unfair. An unreasoned affinity
or purposeful misrepresentation that
prevents objective consideration.

Pew Research Center Report July 22, 2019
*Trust and Distrust in America: Americans' struggles
with truth, accuracy, and accountability.*
**"Many think America is experiencing a crisis in facts
and truth, and they believe this problem ties into the
current state of distrust people have in institutions.
The Center reported that half of U.S. adults say
made-up news and information is a very big problem
in the country today, and about two-thirds say it
causes a great deal of confusion about the basic
facts of current issues and events. Some 61% say the
news media intentionally ignore stories that are
important to the public."**

Entitlement has spawned a new era of contrived truth-
telling, sowing discord between opposing camps. From
their privileged perch, oppressors ramp up rhetoric to
subdue the disadvantaged. In response, the oppressed
spin the truth to justify their cause, demonstrating how

severely they've been marginalized to gain empathy from their advocates. In a reversing stratagem, the oppressed spin the truth to justify their cause, demonstrating how severely they're being victimized to gain empathy from their advocates.

Victim versus victors: it's no longer about ethics, principle, or doing the right thing – it's about sound bites, spin, and narrative to claim victimhood and special considerations.

The marginalization that goads entitlement is essentially a power play by self-proclaimed judges. These power brokers supercharge their sovereignty by misrepresenting reality, consumed with projecting the right optics rather than living with the correct principles. The bias, the twisting of truth and the masquerading of opinion as fact is even more insidious and destructive than the art of canceling folks, as it can have a larger impact when these fallacies are embraced, played, and weaponized worldwide by co-conspiring mainstream media.

We get most news from mainstream and social media. Both are patently biased, ubiquitous, and pervasive. News outlets mix fact with opinion, reporting not truth but spin that endorses their producer's views.

Media masters attract attention by using click baited, provocative tactics to grow viewership while surrendering journalistic integrity. A Gallup/Knight Foundation study found trust in news media hit a record low in 2020. It is the first time in 40 years that Americans with no confidence in mainstream media outnumbered those with at least some confidence. The study revealed Americans feel the news media pushes an agenda favoring business interests over public service.

Media communication is biased, and we perpetuate this bias through warped interpretations shaped by our paradigms, mindsets, and prejudices. Reality is twisted at both ends – biased data input on one end and warped information processing on the other. Over time, the overwhelming amount of negative and biased noise permeating mainstream and social media has turned our natural curiosity into skepticism. Healthy skepticism is good, given the plethora of vehement hyperbole online.

However, when exposed to disparaging content, twisted facts, deluded opinions, and emotional machinations online, we harden from being skeptics (doubters) to cynics (disbelievers). Then you rationalize things by forming and expressing our own opinions as an active critic. Then it gets ugly. You have now entered the fray; you have earned your membership card in today's clash culture.

Depending on how vehement your voice, you may face coalitions that consider you a heretic. You are lambasted as scandalous, blasphemous, and worse. You might think that your contrary ideas are encouraged under the welcome mat of diversity of opinion. But instead, you are hatefully ostracized for voicing non-aligned views. It has reasonable people asking, "Why all the hate?!"

Unfortunately, all that animosity can turn you into a chronic neurotic. Our exposure to unabashed bias and online vitriol contributes to the rapid increase in adolescent depression and suicide.

Accuracy and integrity are further crippled by cell-phones in the hands of regular Joe reporters. The world is now replete with a legion of cell phone-toting private citizen reporters capturing their perspectives on various events. The full standard of veracity – the truth, the whole truth, and nothing but the truth – is nowhere near exhibited in most cases. Individual reporters hide behind anonymity on social platforms in ways legacy media cannot.

When Joe reporter, or his homies are transgressed, for example, when a police officer appears to issue aggressive demands or use physicality to restrain, the intrepid reporter has his spin to share in recounting the events. Of course, there is no way to verify the accurate telling of cellphone-streamed news, as there are numerous ways to distort what truly happened. Most importantly, Joe reporter has no professional or ethical obligation to capture an unbiased truth.

As crimes are reported on phone cameras, political leaders or celebrities are caught publicly saying things that are insulting or offensive in private, as anonymously posted videos of twisted manifestos or rantings and ravings are captured for the world to see- we wake up to a harsh reality. There is a lot of bad stuff going on in the world.

Cell phone video capturing of mistreatment, margin-alization, or improper persecution lights a fire of resentment across large segments of American society. That resentment, rooted first in the realization that persecution exists, is amplified by the speculation that it had been hidden from us for all the years leading up to when cell phones became commonplace. It's as if we were blind and accustomed to that plight, and then our eyes were opened to a biased view of the world, having us appalled at the very thought that all this ugly stuff could ever exist to the degree we now see it. Going from blind to duped somehow doesn't feel like progress.

Bias is also embedded in the social media platforms as they are not equal opportunity endorsers of opinion. Hate speech and dangerous messages are rightfully banned; tragically, though, many voices are silenced because of political persuasion. Though they don't confess unless challenged, social media tech giants can ban or silence as they see fit. Most folks feel the only bias is weeding out right from wrong, when often it's right from left.

Platforms don't fervently protect free speech; they're commonly policed to stifle certain voices. Elon Musk's Twitter files exposed how deep the bias tree's roots go, and they go all the way to federal government agencies.

> *It's as if we were made blind and accustomed to that plight, and then our eyes were opened to a biased view of the world, having us appalled at the very thought that all this ugly stuff could ever exist.*

Political correctness jeopardizes the veracity of news reporting; we can't call a spade a spade. The prevailing sentiment around victimhood and inequity has infiltrated the messages of mainstream media. For years, the media has been reluctant to use condemning labels, despite their accuracy, to remain politically correct.

Perpetrators of crime are often painted as victims! Victims of an unfair system that made them act badly. As Thomas Paine said in *Common Sense:* "Long habit of not thinking a thing Wrong, gives it a superficial appearance of being Right."

Why does mainstream media buy into and perpetuate a prejudiced worldview espousing victimhood, canonizing group identity, and advocating for government overreach? Because mainstream media lives off the bad news of inequities derived from human frailty. Watch. In any TV newscast, virtually all stories showcase the bad side, except maybe the obligatory feel-good closing item.

Broadcasters feature bad and often shocking news because it's what their audience wants. People often feel relieved when watching bad news because it makes them feel better about their own lives, knowing their own lives aren't as bad as those of the hapless victims.

Many years ago, a California news station attempted to broadcast exclusively good news. It lasted only a few weeks because nobody tuned in. TV producers put out content people want to see, stuff that enhances ratings, which is what keeps them on the air.

A 2018 Pew Research study found that two-thirds of Americans think that made-up news and altered videos create confusion about the facts. The same report states that social media companies have too much control over the news mix on their platforms.

While Americans have faith in their ability to recognize misleading information, they're less sure about the ability of others. An overwhelming 83% say one-sided and inaccurate news is a very big or moderately big problem on social media.

To frame today's perceived reality with our preferred spin, we've fallen into rewriting history and laying waste to the grand purpose for which our country was formed. This bias toward unpatriotic, un-American thought targets the most vulnerable: our children.

Schools are ravaged by misinformation, which distorts history and promotes false notions of acceptable behavior and morals. If a child embraces Critical Race Theory, for example, then that child could be convinced that Americans are bad people bent on manipulating and ravaging the vulnerable.

That mentality has our young students denigrate the valor of our Founding Fathers and disrespect the service of many of our early Presidents solely based on past transgressions borne of the culture of the time. Teaching kids they are bad people born of bad people, descending from bad people, is clearly not good.

From an early age to adulthood, our kids are being reprogrammed at school. Grade schoolers no longer say the Pledge of Allegiance. High school students learn from sports heroes to disrespect the flag. From kindergarten to diploma, kids are indoctrinated with guilt over our country's supposedly sordid past.

A parent's primary job is to raise their children to become responsible adults. You can tell by the hostility exchanged between parents and school board administrators that most parents feel they are fighting an uphill battle over curriculum and narrative versus common sense. It makes little sense to tell our children fables and stories of knights in shining armor —fictional heroes — while denigrating the true heroes of our past.

That approach reinforces the idea that there are no real heroes, and by inference, heroic deeds are beyond the potential of real people. Heroic nature is being stifled. We need a next generation of heroes, not indoctrinated wimps and dummies.

Within and beyond the walls of our schools, traditions and history are under siege. Historical figures are disenfranchised; statues are torn down, portraits are removed, books are banned, and stories are untruthfully retold because yesterday's moral standards don't square with today's. We should learn from and celebrate our past rather than denigrate it. Our past is our past and cannot be changed, or we risk stripping away part of who we are, part of our identity.

By denigrating past heroes' contemptible deeds, even though heavily influenced by the culture of the day and not representative of the hero's essence, history rewriters earn their own special merit badge for being above past misdeeds, for discrediting and posturing superiority over historical figures. This is the phenomenon called Virtue Signaling.

Virtue signaling soothes the ego of wimps unable to take responsibility and seek self-worth. They denigrate others in favor of the oppressed in the fake role of a masked Lone Ranger coming to the rescue. These Lone Rangers or Social Justice Warriors (SJWs) look to ride their high horse by redefining justice itself. Justice is justice, but under their emancipator guise, SJWs refer to social justice, racial justice, environmental justice, or gender justice. When a limiting descriptor modifies 'justice,' the concept is no longer pure; it takes on the full force of agenda-driven narrative.

Social justice had gone mainstream in its fakery. Media bias has morphed into false reporting or silencing significant news stories to religiously play to a favored spin. We've added narrative, optics, fake news, and fact-checking to more regular use of words like conspiracy and lies. Prevarications became so common that a federal Disinformation Governance Board was formed, then disbanded due to push back on the panel's inability to be truthful and unbiased!

As people increasingly hunger for bad news, conspiracy theories have seen a marked increase. In the 20th century, a few conspiracy theories got traction. Today, a new conspiracy theory emerges every other week, claiming victimhood and shifting the responsibility onto external forces.

The most captivating conspiracies center on faceless, sinister, amorphous dark forces. Believing the source is ghostlike deepens the conspiracy; ghosts can't be confronted, intimidated, or brought to justice. Listen to demagogues and their "bogeyman" stories. These tales are spun because they're effective. The protagonist ghosts exist and continue haunting with impunity, bound only by the emergence of another zombie manifestation of darkness.

Virtue signaling soothes the ego of wimps unable to take responsibility and seek self-worth. They denigrate others in favor of the oppressed in the fake role of a masked Lone Ranger coming to the rescue.

There's a lot of untruth-telling going on, beyond conspiracy conjecture, spinning deep into half-truths, twisted truth, intentional omissions, deliberate deceptions, and bald-faced lies. Jordan Peterson, Canadian psychologist, author, and social critic, in a YouTube commentary about the dangers of totalitarianism: "You know people think that when you're in a totalitarian state the reason that the state is totalitarian because everyone is the victim of top-down pressure from tyrants and that's completely, that's not how it works at all... a state becomes totalitarian when every single person is lying about absolutely everything all the time."

Let's put that on a bumper sticker: "Shameless disregard for truth proliferates as a corruptible power!"

Untruth-telling is becoming pervasive and divisive. This dismantling of truth is most destructive when it works from the bottom up, taking hold within our young adult population—those most impressionable, most ardently searching for truth and meaning, who most vehemently and naively promulgate ideology in all directions.

Clearly, the pervasive, patently biased reporting of mainstream news, the expression of provocative opinions, and the assembly of convenient data and 'facts' are creating a falsified knowledge base. Opposing sides are moving further to extreme positions to gain attention. As a result, our nation has never been more divided philosophically and socially. The biased narrative appears to be heavily flavored and tailored to suit political tastes and personal agendas. Bias has shifted the truth at the center, moving it simultaneously hard to the left and hard to the right.

Fake news and rumors thrive online because few verify what's real and always **Bias** towards content that reinforces their own biases.

— Ryan Higa

As we formulate the truth, what becomes essential isn't The Truth but our reality, our Truth, our identity. Because identity today is heavily tied to group identity, we yearn for the real human part of existence: individualism. To overcome the increasingly onerous grip of group identity and the coercive nature of biased truth-telling, many folks double down on their individual claims to personal reality. They focus on significance and become obsessed with their persona, totally consumed with themselves and how others view them.

Unfortunately, the self-centered focus is usually on image rather than character, personal brand rather than real identity, form rather than substance, skin-deep rather than deep down inside. Image and outward appearance have accelerated from a mere fancy to an interest and now to a full-time Obsession.

Questions to Ponder:

1. In this age of instant access to biased information sources, in what ways has truth been devalued?
2. If virtue signaling is dishonest, how does one best advocate for others?

Technology
Identity
Marginalization
Entitlement
Bias
Obsession

Chapter 17

Obsession

An idea or thought that continually preoccupies a person's mind; A persistent, disturbing preoccupation with an often-unreasonable idea or feeling.

PsychTests AIM Inc. April 12, 2022
Self-centered People are Unhappy People – New Study digs into the personality of egoists

With data from 12,259 individuals, PsychTests' researchers examined traits of people who say they only look out for themselves ("Self-Servers") and compared them to others who balance their own needs and interests with those of others ("Balancers"). Findings were as follows:

Self-Servers tend to have a cynical view:
- 50% of Self-Servers are proclaimed pessimists vs. 20% of Balancers.
- 53% feel that other people take advantage of them vs. 20% of Balancers.

Self-Servers are more likely to believe that:
- You should only help someone if it benefits you in some way 37% vs. 1%
- In order to get ahead, you have to step on a few toes 57% vs. 11%.

The average Joe believes that rather than trust in the whim of bias, it is better to establish a personal truth by capitalizing on one's own personal brand and image. As a result, the typical TikTok or Instagram aficionado is obsessed with themselves, their image, and their looks, with the sole objective of garnering attention, likes, and followers. The year 2014 was declared the Year of the Selfie, and today, more than 90 million selfies are taken daily.

Quite simply, we are obsessed with our looks, not our beliefs, not our principles, nor our virtues, but rather our physical looks. Quite sad.

We're also obsessed with how others look. A relatively new platform for soft porn is OnlyFans, where guys obsessed with carnal desire get so caught up that they pay to view despite ready access to all sorts of free, provocative images or videos on the internet. Where there is a ready market for making easy money, street walkers, Only Fans virtual brothel owners, or other debauchery-enabled profiteers will take that path. Image and money seem to matter more than morals in this age of obsession.

There's a related phenomenon with the general elevation of female promiscuity that's held to be liberating for the women involved, but the reality is much different. It's actually a form of oppression that many of the women themselves only realize years later. Left to our own devices, this and related types of moral degradation are likely to get worse.

And yes, even the morally centered among us have become obsessed with self-image, meticulously curating their look with Photoshop and featuring only the highlight reels of their lives, hustling a provocativeness that will garner more views on social platforms.

We have become a society of narcissists. And for those who don't play, the price tag is FOMO induced depression as the faked perfect lives of the narcissists parade across their computer screens. The obsession with looks, with image, runs deep, so much so that there is an overdose of sympathy for those who are not blessed with traditional good looks.

Overweight and out-of-shape models who were once 'marginalized' are now featured in magazines to promote real-world, unabashed beauty. The majority embracing the liberated view of beauty are simply pretentious virtue signalers who feel an obligation to flaunt their fake right-eousness. Image is not what we see but what we are conditioned to see. In the case of overweight models, beauty is not in the eye of the beholder but rather in a beholden air of haughtiness.

All the posturing has us praise the undeserving, which, of course, makes it all a Pyrrhic or hollow victory, with the surface-level applause more than squelched by the deep-down inside feeling of guilt that can well up from the unearned praise.

The obsession with image to get attention also has many folks doing outlandish things on social platforms to garner views. Posts have become increasingly provocative in an effort to generate a viral response (yes, it's a disheartening disease). This one-upmanship is spiraling out of control, with kids dying while performing online challenges – a new-age 'double dog dare ya'.

Related to all this self-promotion is an obsession with celebrity—those Hollywood favorites, sports champions, and most listened-to pundits whom we love to love, if nothing else, for their fame.

Today, on social platforms, anyone can become somebody if they are lucky enough, bold enough, or provocative enough to post something that gets people talking. And it can go viral if it is outlandish or fantastic enough to weaponize extremes of the full spectrum of emotion, from fury to frenzy.

Fame is traditionally defined as "the state of being known or recognized by many people because of your achievements or skill, etc.; of a favorable character; renown". Sadly, the 'fame' that viral posters seek is usually without substance, and in many cases, that is the rub. It's a game of deception with identity playing out as a masquerade.

The obsession game has now gone professional. Professional, vanity-fueled exhibitionists known as influencers go to great lengths to keep regular folks tuned in to their antics, undeserved fame, and absurd self-centeredness. A whole army of protégé attention grabbers is following in the footsteps of the Kardashian-Jenner clan, Paris Hilton, and their successors. It seems we have shifted from living our own lives to watching other people's, often fake ones at that.

Our fixation on the antics of online exhibitionists is clearly evident in the 90-9-1 rule of social media networks. Generally, only 1 percent of online users actively create content, while another 9 percent participate by commenting, rating, or sharing the content. The vast majority, the remaining 90 percent, are entranced in a watch, look, and read-only mode.

Another obsessive behavior phenomenon has recently struck the women's cosmetics industry. In popular beauty store outlets like Sephora and Ulta, this curious spectacle has been dubbed "Sephora Kids." Customers of these in-vogue beauty chains are voicing their displeasure with a disturbing trend that is upending the normal decorum of their cosmetic counters. Sephora kids, those pre-teens, typically girls between 9 and 12 years of age, inspired by their online influencer heroes, barge into cosmetic stores with wild abandon, deploying mean girl antics and displaying an overabundance of entitlement.

Regular customers complain that these Sephora Kids are rude, pushy and insist on being served first. These young girls are often seen making a mess of the store's counters, ripping into sealed products without buying them.

In addition to ruining the experience for regular shoppers, Sephora Kids burden their accompanying parents as well by employing Machiavellian tactics to strong-arm them into buying whatever they want right now, with it all playing out in a tantrum-like manner.

What the Sephora Kids show is their warped sense of entitlement and acquired affliction of looks obsession. They're pushy and insist on special treatment so they can flash the look of their influencer trendsetters. They lay waste to the orderliness of product displays upsetting others with their spoiled attitude and rude shenani-gans. Understandably, many Sephora and Ulta customers are calling for cosmetic stores to impose an age restriction that would ban anyone under age 18 from entering.

The obsession game has now gone profes-sional. Professional, vanity-fueled exhibi-tionists known as influencers go to great lengths to keep regular folks tuned in to their antics, undeserved fame, and absurd self-centeredness.

Today's younger generation of social platform surfers idolize celebrities and glamorize influencers. That is all wrong for a couple of reasons. There should be no idol-atry of any earthly thing or person.

Our heroes should inspire us to move our lives forward and serve as role models for the person we dream of becoming - that person we can grow into, who makes a positive difference in the world. Celebrity culture, however, is all wrong with a misdirection of aspi-ration and motivation. Losers idolize narcissists and blowhards, while winners strive to emulate true heroes. A January 2024 opinion piece written by Michael Levin titled "If you can't Name a half-decent Role Model, you can't work here" provides some insight. Mr. Levin reports on an employer in Sweden that asks a qualifying ques-tion of potential hires to gauge their values. The question is this: "Aside from family members, who are your role models?"

Levin is surprised by what he hears as he reports, "To a shockingly high degree, the interviewees can't answer the question." He goes on to say, "They can't think of a single human being they view as a role model, with the possible exception of climate activist Greta Thunberg, whose name comes up frequently."

Michael Levin then asks, "Why do so many job seekers cite Greta Thunberg? The overwhelming career aspiration among young people is to become an influencer. In secular Europe, climate action is practically a religion. So, according to the Swedish CEO, Thunberg is a modern-day Joan of Arc, combining classical idealism with the modern-day urge to get "likes.""

In the article, Mr. Levin reflects on the past, suggesting that reasonable answers to that same question years ago would have come quickly to mind... names like JFK, Martin Luther King, Winston Churchill, or Henry Ford. Mr. Levin then ponders the concept of role models and how our views have changed over time. "All we think about is what's trending, not what's lasting." He adds "Our devices increase our sense of self-importance far out of proportion to who we really are. My phone. My feed. My timeline. My profile. My, my, my. It's all about me, so what do I need a role model for?"

In citing another contributing cause of this phenomenon, Mr. Levin echoes one of the earlier points herein: that, in this internet and cell phone age, we simply have too much information about people, events, and others' opinions. When we know too much, when we are privy to laudable things heroes have done as well as their indiscretions, foibles, and private mistakes, we struggle in holding them in high esteem.

He sums things up in his article by saying, "On top of that, the world just looks too big, its problems too intractable, to make a difference. The Earth's climate, the political climate, the social climate… it all seems impossible to fix. So why bother?"

In our got-to- have-it-now culture there is great resistance to investing time and effort today if the payoff is long past tomorrow. Wanting something right now can arise from intense desire, but it signals obsession when it's intrusive, persistent, causes significant anxiety, interferes with daily life, or involves a compulsive need to control or possess the object of desire. It moves from normal wanting to obsession when that urge becomes a disruptive, uncontrollable preoccupation that dictates your mood and actions, often leading to distress rather than pleasure. Where in your experience have you seen obsessive behavior impacting people's lives?

Many years ago, social scientists led by psychologist Walter Mischel conducted a study on delayed gratification that later became known as the "Stanford Marshmallow Experiment". In this study, a child was offered a choice between one small but immediate reward (a marshmallow on a plate) or two rewards (two marshmallows) if they refrained from eating the first one, having waited for a specified period of time. Video recordings of the kids sitting by themselves, isolated in a room with a reserved marshmallow sitting on a plate in front of them, are quite entertaining.

During the experiment, observers noted a decline in temptation resistance in the expressions and movements of the subjects. They saw squirming, fidgeting and eyes scanning the room to ensure secrecy. As this was a tough test for most 5-year-olds, the majority succumbed to the temptation.

Interestingly, the social scientists followed up with the test subjects many years later and found that the kids who resisted the temptation and earned a second marshmallow had achieved more in life. Indeed, it has been learned that the ability to delay gratification is a reliable marker of personal success.

For the observant among us, it would be apropos to view the marshmallow experiment as a microcosm of our modern world. Most obviously, treats offered by the generous experimenters are symbolic of the temptations that are quite accessible in our society. The limited number of choices and favorable payoffs is consistent with the scarcity mindset most folks are encumbered with today.

Furthermore, the framework of the experiment, which involves a subject and an unseen observer, is symbolic of our digital world, where big tech algorithms unobtrusively monitor every action we take. The cold, hard reality of reward waiting only for those unyielding to instant gratification quite accurately models a principal precept of our real world.

And finally, the kids' excuses or pleading of innocence at the end of the experiment, despite sticky fingers and empty plate evidence, is representative of a void of honesty and responsibility that is filled with scapegoating and begging for unearned benefits, as encouraged by our society of entitlement. It's a dog-eat-dog and kid-eat-marshmallow world out there.

Obsession is the single most wasteful human activity, because with an obsession you keep coming back and back and back to the same question and never get an answer.

— *Norman Mailer*

As we obsess over our online reputation and go for the limelight, putting ourselves out there, we become vulnerable. Everything that we do online, revealing our life stories, makes our personal information accessible to others.

Personal content privacy is unfortunately not one of the perks of being so open about ourselves on social networks. Yet, we knowingly and obsessively share our secrets despite the risk of evil-doers playing on the web, hijacking content we had hoped others saw but not them.

In stealth mode, our personal information, including not just the content we post, but also our search and purchase behavior, as well as the global positioning coordinates of our every step, is being recorded in our digital footprint. Armed with this information, a cartel of personal information hijackers conspires to defraud you, to use insidious means to get you to buy their stuff that you don't need and to manipulate you. The more obsessed you are, the more vulnerable you are to Manipulation.

Questions to Ponder:

1. What in this world is worth obsessing over?
2. How does an obsession with looks, fame or money affect individuals or groups of people?

Technology
Identity
Marginalization
Entitlement
Bias
Obsession
Manipulation

Chapter 18
Manipulation

Controlling someone or something
to your own advantage, often unfairly
or dishonestly, and in many cases,
in a stealthy or clandestine manner.

"Filtering on Facebook can make it hard for people to see ideas other than their own, and they can form extremely radical viewpoints. Fragmented realities based on false information deepen the existing cleavages within the society and hinder the mobilization of the people. In addition to filtering, the use of deep fakes and bots to manipulate people by the data they provide is another challenge AI poses to the integrity of democracy. The 2016 US elections, as well as the Brexit referendum manipulations from Cambridge Analytica, are only two examples of many more, where fair elections are harder to achieve in a digitalized world where perception control is a reality both from other authoritarian regimes as well as from our government. Creating a double-edged sword for people to be manipulated."

As our lives proliferate online, more and more information about us becomes accessible to others. Without us taking much notice, our personal information is being intercepted and gathered through tech platforms that record our personal story, our every move, our physical location at any point in time, our actions, our searches, and our purchases.

The privacy pirates exploit the unsuspecting, using the stolen data for their own nefarious purposes. Their manipulation starts with the stealing of your personal information and then progresses into identity theft. It happens more often than you may think.

On the identity theft crime log: Yahoo 2013 – 3 billion records affected; Equifax 2017 – 148 million records affected; Facebook 2019- 540 million records affected; Microsoft 2021 – 38 million records affected. And, of course, smaller, more targeted breaches occur every day. From 2020 through 2025 more than 6 million cases of identity theft were reported to the FTC. Unfortunately, there is a real market need for identity theft protection and reputation management services today.

Beware, information shared becomes data hijacked, which then becomes the fodder for manipulation. Even information not shared can be hijacked as well, as many corporate chief executives who have had to pay ransoms to retrieve stolen company proprietary information can attest.

And it's not just a one-way street. To use all weapons at their disposal, the manipulating information hounds funnel content in the opposite direction, from their power-broker perch, disseminating propaganda to the unwitting to influence and incite. When wielded by hellhounds with incendiary language and a thirst for power and evil intent, the result can be online radicalization of regular, commonsensical folk who are ensnared in their lair.

Things have changed over the years. In the 1960s and 1970s, we received nearly all our news from a few newspapers and three television networks. Back then, honest, reliable news coverage was the product. Beginning in the 80s and 90s, dozens of new news outlets joined in and jockeyed for market share, transforming the product from news reporting to provocative, attention-grabbing storytelling. TV news since that time has deteriorated into being increasingly sensational, making it hard to distinguish between real news and fake news. Somewhere along the way journalism has become activism.

Now, with hi-tech video editing tools like Photoshop, Deepfake, and AI being used to capitalize on fakery, for example, by real kidnappers who mimic voices of loved ones, it is getting incredibly challenging and life-impacting to determine what is real and what is not.

The social platforms have toiled endlessly to enroll new participants, grow viewership, and maximize the time people spend on their virtual pages. The more time folks spend, the greater the opportunity to make an indelible impact on impressionable minds.

Information shared becomes data hijacked, which then becomes the fodder for manipulation.

In social experiments, sociologists have discovered that specific actions, combined with intermittent rewards, can create an addictive dopamine rush. Taking advantage of both the dopamine rush and the preconditioning effect (Pavlov's dogs salivating at the sound of a bell), social network designers use stimuli in the form of audible and visual alerts to spike our dopamine levels upon the receipt of emails, text messages, or tweets.

Our advanced technology serves as a portal to shirked responsibility and squelched ambition. The dopamine-seeking behavior leads to listlessness, laziness, and feelings of loneliness. In the past decade, depression and anxiety levels of young adults have risen to epidemic proportions.

Former social platform executives have expressed concerns over the manipulative programming of users. Sean Parker and Chamath Palihapitiya, leaders in Facebook's early years, have been critical of exploiting vulnerabilities in human psychology. In interviews now on YouTube, Sean Parker, the first President of Facebook has said "It's a social validation feedback loop that, it's like, I mean, it's exactly the kind of thing that a hacker like myself would come up with because you are exploiting a vulnerability in human psychology." Parker added "God only knows what it is doing to our children's brains."

Chamath Palihapitiya, who led new user growth and oversaw Facebook's growth to over 1 billion users, said in YouTube interviews, "You don't know, but you are being programmed" and "Social media is ripping apart society."

In a 2011 interview with The New York Times shortly before he passed away, Steve Jobs said he banned his kids from using Apple's new product, the iPad, saying in his own words, "We don't allow the iPad in the home. We think it's too dangerous for them."

At the 16th annual Oslo Freedom Forum in 2024, Jack Dorsey, co-founder of Twitter, expressed concern about the power of algorithms embedded in platforms. "I think the free speech debate is a complete distraction right now. The real debate should be about free will. We are being programmed based on what we say we're interested in."

Scary stuff from the tech moguls who might as well have parroted Captain Robert Lewis, co-pilot of the Enola Gay, when he penned in his journal just after releasing the atomic bomb on the city of Hiroshima, "My God, what have we done?"

What we have done is create a bewitching online environment where perspectives are warped and reasoning is subverted. At each click and scroll, we are exposed to content that plays like a series of cartoons. Some online content is innocuous entertainment, but far too much is alluring, salacious and vile content, with hyperbolic fantasy violence thrown in. It is having serious repercussions. Numerous lawsuits being filed against AI providers whose chatbots encourage self-harm and suicide among teens flag a clear and present danger.

Even live video coverage of horrific events feels unreal, as if in another universe or on a perpetual sequel of *"Hunger Games"* where death is viewed as entertainment. Violent content that major legacy media historically would not broadcast now appears in your social media feed, accompanied by an advisory that does nothing but entice you to watch it repeatedly and share it with 'friends.'

Some online content is innocuous entertainment, but far too much is alluring, salacious and vile content, with hyperbolic fantasy violence thrown in.

Beyond the social media giants, advertisers also play the mind programming game well. Television interrupts millions of viewers with repetitive messages, a powerful license to influence and manipulate. Now, advertisers monitor your every move to see what gets your attention. In the process, they skillfully trigger pop-up ads and promotional messages to whet your appetite for purchase.

The title of sociologist and author Shoshana Zuboff's

best-selling book says it all, *The Age of Surveillance Capitalism.* Have you ever noticed that just after a conversation with a friend on an infrequent topic, you then see ads on your social media pages for exactly that same thing?

Your smart tech devices are listening to you!

Try a Google search like "American history is..." or "The key to your success is..." You will most often receive responses that align with your perspective. Search algorithms manipulate by surveilling and reinforcing sentiment through resharing and supercharging views of their unwary prey. Additionally, institutional surveillance, the disturbing type reminiscent of Big Brother of George Orwell's book, *1984,* appears to be proliferating offline (in our real world). Indeed, recent lawsuits against big-box retailers for not obtaining patron permission for using biometric data from facial recognition scans are consistent with this fear. Kinda scary.

Manipulation also comes from individuals who exploit the power of the internet for personal gain. The most common source of manipulation comes from the vanguard of 'victims' who guilt-shame anyone who does not kowtow to their cause. These opinion brokers manipulate guilt. These crybullies, in complaining about being offended or victimized, manipulate sentiment to attack and silence their imagined oppressors.

Manipulation online plays from four suits in the manipulator's deck: Reward, Ideology, Coercion, & Ego.

The 4 motivators activated in Manipulation:

- **Reward:** Money, praise, other positive bounty, gifts, or freebies
- **Ideology:** What folks believe in. Their core convictions, articles of faith, views, customs, and opinions
- **Coercion:** Forced by guilt, blackmail, threats, intimidation, and bullying
- **Ego:** Driven by self-interest - wanting to be perceived a certain way, exuding pride, motivated by vanity, and being narcissistic.

Social media provides an opportunity to manipulate based on every motivator. There is a reward waiting for influencers, a chance to voice beliefs, and a risk of those beliefs being ridiculed. Coercion takes ridicule further with intimidation and bullying. And of course, the platforms are perfect venues for self-promotion, selfies, and ego-soothing displays.

Beyond the average Joe, there is a cadre of conspirators and exploiters who take the whole manipulation game to the next level. These power brokers are captains of industry, leaders of countries, and influential politicians who seize whatever power they can muster to advance their agendas. They are country leaders, heads of government, leaders of major businesses, and institutional leaders.

Take heed of the often-clandestine nature of the

manipulator's power. Power does not necessarily corrupt; it reveals the heart. And the more secrets an unscrupulous heart conceals, the greater the potential for manipulation.

The modus operandi of authoritarian regimes is to wield power by eliminating opposition, sowing discord, and controlling through fearmongering. Once a critical mass of fear is instilled, the tyrants push their agenda to weaponize power and foment violence, through self-serving dogma.

When those who hold dominion are accused of abusing their power, they often enlist supporters. Propaganda campaigners, political pundits, lobbyists, and media outlets often enter the fray. The goal is to hijack the conscience and sentiments of the public, stoking the fires of division by playing to tribal sensitivities through identity politics.

Be wary, those in power are likely manipulating you to prevent you from questioning their actions. With great fervor, they will claim that all the accusations against them are conspiracy theories.

Our First Amendment guarantee to freedom of speech is under attack as criminalization of free speech takes hold. Free speech comes at a cost. It pays to be vigilant in every corner of the online world, to be alert to the ever-present bullies whose courage comes from being hidden behind a screen.

Online manipulation is ubiquitous. The targets of manipulation are often discombobulated to the point of questioning their sense of reality and truth. We now have

a term for this type of psychological manipulation –
gaslighting.

When you're surrounded by a world of constant lies, **Manipulation**, and deceit, that dark energy is bound to seep into you eventually.

— *Jeffrey Bowyer-Chapman*

It is becoming increasingly difficult to distinguish fact from fiction and accurate reporting from spin. The multitude of manipulating narratives gives rise to an attitude of "so what" and makes people question what is important and what isn't.

The twisted untruth-telling epidemic born of postured virtuosity has the masses questioning their own beliefs as the manipulating power brokers look to do the nasty...reprogram our beliefs... to turn upside down what we have long felt or known to be fundamental in our real world.

Manipulation is turned into a monster when it attacks our personal and defining foundational Beliefs.

Questions to Ponder:

1. In what way is manipulation still unacceptable

even if the 'victim' doesn't perceive any negative impact on themselves?

2. What evidence is there today of an oppressive 'Big Brother' who uses tech to stifle voices, corrupt information, and use language for mind control?

Technology
Identity
Marginalization
Entitlement
Bias
Obsession
Manipulation
Belief

Chapter 19

Belief

Trust, faith, or confidence in someone
or something. Something that is
accepted or considered to be true.

Gallup Poll November, 2023 by Frank Newport
Measuring Trends in Americans' Personal Values

<u>Religion</u>
On the question of "How important would you say religion is in your daily life?" 61% responded "very important" in 1998; only 44% said the same in 2023, a 17-point decline in 25 years.
<u>Patriotism</u>
Americans were asked how proud they are to be an American.
In 2023, 39% of Americans reported being extremely proud to be an American, while 28% were very proud—a decline from 55% in 2001.
<u>Community</u>
Gallup's 2023 poll showed that 18% of Americans consider community activities "extremely important," with 37% considering them "very important," placing this at the very bottom of the list of issues polled.

It's not what you think...
It's what you believe that matters.

With misinformation, bias, marginalization, entitlement, and manipulation swirling around us, what can we hold as honorable and true? Most people rely on the undeniable core of who they are, their identity, and foundational beliefs. Identity is intertwined with our beliefs and values. Indeed, our identity is a form of belief. Yet, today, our collective beliefs have become scattered, shifting rapidly as values lose their anchor. With societal norms in flux and political correctness demanding equal deference to all viewpoints, our belief system is morphing at a startling pace.

Today, it is volatile and conflicting beliefs and values that are pulling us apart... not ill-informed, impressionistic views of the political landscape. What was once a fairly stable set of beliefs is now crumbling apart like a stale old cookie. Many are searching for purpose but failing to find it, and a culture of entitlement has eroded our sense of meaning. Purpose, our highest form of belief, is being replaced by a willingness to float along as oppressed victims, squandering our potential. It seems that we are offended by everything yet empowered by nothing.

Our belief system, our view of what is fundamentally true in our world, is under attack from a variety of transgressors. Concerning well-being alone, we're facing unprecedented levels of harm. As alarming as it sounds, we are killing ourselves at an unprecedented rate.

Drug overdose deaths reflect a deepening desperation, as a loss of meaning and purpose drives many toward drugs to numb the pain or chase a dopamine rush. Overdose deaths rose from 6.8 per 100,000 in 2001 to 32.4 in 2021!

Drug overdose deaths are a canary-in-the-coal- mine harbinger of a morbid reality, the reality of a dangerous level of desperation and despair in our country today.

And for mainstream America there too are killers, subtle and dangerous, lurking at every turn. Our middle school and high school kids increasingly face shaming, bullying, and marginalization online, fueling depression and suicide. The suicide rate for youth and young adults ages 10 to 24 increased 60% from 2011 to 2021. Let that sink in.

Moreover, the increased level of depression and suicide among the young has not abated in the past few years as the COVID-19 pandemic spiked anxiety levels for all age groups.

COVID-19 amplified the damage. Its impact was not just physical but psychological – confusion, loneliness, and fear drove people to cling to "the science," even as the science was evolving and incomplete. Unfortunately, the science of pandemics like COVID was and still is so poorly developed that the knowledge void was filled by folks sharing their chosen version of the evolving science that conformed to their political and social beliefs. Beliefs can be twisted in many different ways, but perhaps most insidiously when belief bandits capitalize on public anxiety, shaping perceptions for their own ends.

A similar dynamic has played out with Climate Change, where underdeveloped science has been used to spread predictions of imminent doom. Power brokering raiders of reason and belief bandits thrive on confusion and the recklessness of irreverence to common sense. It puts us all at their mercy. It raises the questions: are we losing faith in the disciplined pursuit of truth? Do we increasingly view ourselves as victims of forces beyond our control?

Our worldview colors everything we experience. Far too many view life through dark-tinted lenses. In addition to these dark tinters there is a large crowd who choose to see things through light adaptive life lenses... you know, the lenses that, by design, suppress true light. Invariably, both groups are continually searching for a clear and fundamental understanding, often turning to modern science, which continues to evolve and correct itself, aiming to be the ultimate authority.

But science is only as strong as the questions we dare ask and can answer. As soon as we think we've figured it all out, we're reminded that vast unknowns remain. Multiverses anyone?

Not yet knowing and then striving to learn through the scientific method is a natural and productive thing. However, when manipulators, raiders of reason and belief bandits, look to brutalize belief capitalizing on the gaps in scientific knowledge for things like Covid and Climate, inventing their own rules of cause and effect to prey on the unknowing... well that is a den of danger.

Beyond science, beyond our physical and biological world environment, our social belief system is mutating too. A University of Chicago poll showed that only 67 % of respondents believe hard work is very important. A growing number of young adults are embracing "lying flatism," a lifestyle originating in China that advocates a minimalist approach, doing the bare minimum just to get by.

Indeed, it may be accurate to suggest that younger generations today are more inclined than past generations to strive to succeed in their own slow-paced, passive and pampered way, hoping that the stars align and that their lives find good fortune and fall into favor. Lying flatism is a laissez-faire approach to life- one that adds to the delayed adulthood chapter of a younger generation's book of growing up, not today, but tomorrow.

The same University of Chicago poll showed a significant decline in values traditionally held in high regard. When asked if they highly value traditionally important things, respondents in that poll said 'Yes' at these alarming low rates: Patriotism: 38%, Religion: 39%, Having Children: 30%, Community Involvement: 26%.

To sum it up for you, less than half of the younger generation loves this country, less than half believes in God (or in something greater than themselves), less than half wants children or a family, and less than half wants to be involved in their communities.

Changing mores and mindsets are also illustrated in a Gallup poll of 2021 that found a significant decline in confidence in societal institutions, the Supreme Court, Congress, public schools, mainstream news media and the presidency. That study found increased usage of the term 'systemic' as part of the criticism of institutions such as education, the military industrial complex, the pharmaceutical/medical industry and governmental agencies.

The rise of the word systemic suggests people no longer see isolated failures – they see corruption as embedded and inescapable. Perhaps it is truly the rapid devolution of mores, mindsets and beliefs that is the real systemic scourge in our society.

OMG, not even God is immune to the contagion of declining beliefs. Gallup polls have shown a decline in belief in God, from over 98% believing in 1967, to 92% in 2011, down to 87% in 2017 to 81% in 2022.

Religion through the history of mankind has had a meaningful relationship in an interplay, a dance with science. Albert Einstein once said "Science without religion is lame, religion without science is blind." Indeed, our ancient ancestors had limited science so their religion was blinded by their limited understanding of the heavens. At the other extreme, a mature science and reliance on the same tends to dampen appetite for religiosity and spirituality. Materialism, a science-based world view, minimizes religious or spiritual belief systems leaving no impetus for exploring deeper philosophical questions.

Interesting enough, today we find ourselves at an unusual crossroads in our journey of evolving scientific and religious belief. Both are under scrutiny with belief in both waning as their respective foundational principles are being discounted. Today we scoff at science and we reject religion. Chalk it up to a tsunami of skepticism that pounds our shores as biased truth telling continues to inundate the beachheads of our consciousness.

> ***Perhaps it is truly the rapid devolution of mores, mindsets and beliefs that is the real systemic scourge in our society.***

With the two linchpins of belief – God and Science – destabilized, people seek a belonging in like-minded communities. We long for foundational principles – beliefs that endure. Yet, we remain addicted to technology that entertains, distracts, and connects us in ways that leave us vulnerable and lonely.

In a recent interview, speaking on the topic of an all-embracing power, Jordan Peterson warned of a technology capable of seeing everything – a modern Eye of Sauron, watching endlessly. Peterson said "If you forego your relationship with the omniscient, you'll create a technology that replicates that for you except there will be nothing about it that will be your friend." In the same interview he added, "The fear of God is the beginning of all wisdom."

As we try to understand our place in our world, we spew our philosophy as if it were a religion or grounded firmly in science. The new influencers of belief favor a spin congruent to their favorite narrative aligned to their concocted agenda. In this environment, truth no longer requires a foundation or evidence, because it has become individualized.

With our strong predilection toward self and identity, exploration of truth now has gone inward to the understanding of self. So, it is a matter of not only understanding the truth of the universe but our own invented and professed truth. Truth seeking is truly challenging as everyone has their own sense of reality and their own means and source for validating and expressing beliefs and identity.

Yet, those who can shape societal beliefs wield considerable influence. Those who excel in this area are rewarded. For most folks, though, it is simply the ability to curate and live one's own beliefs that enables any level of fulfillment.

Consider the once-beloved talk show host who built an empire by sharing fundamental truths with uncommon empathy. Eventually, in pursuit of higher ratings, the show platformed fringe beliefs and bizarre philosophies. The once-popular show spiraled into oblivion, and its star moved on.

The lesson? There is The Truth, and then there is Your Truth. For a belief to endure, the two must eventually align and become timeless. Otherwise, dissonance – personal or societal – is inevitable.

One life is all we have and we live it as we believe in living it. But to sacrifice what you are and to live without **Belief**, that is a fate more terrible than dying.

— *Joan of Arc*

Our Beliefs of today vs. yesterday:

Evolving New World Beliefs

1. Because the future holds limited promise, we might as well live for the moment
2. We are all victims of some kind
3. Social circles are more important than the family
4. Being sensitive and emotional are desired attributes for the modern male
5. Career & financial independence should be top goals for the modern woman
6. Sharing the wealth and relying on government trumps capitalism
7. Big corporations are evil, and their leaders are self-serving egotists
8. Equity requires deferring to disenfranchised groups
9. Criticism is equivalent to hate speech
10. Race and gender define human identity

Traditional Beliefs being Displaced

1. Religion /God
2. Personal responsibility for one's livelihood
3. Family as the core social entity
4. A man's presence & leadership at home is vital

5. A woman's natural essence best radiates in motherhood
6. Working hard to be self-sufficient is noble
7. A pioneering and enterprising spirit drives the American Dream
8. Fairness means equal opportunity
9. Freedom of Speech; "Sticks & stones may break my bones, but names will never hurt me"
10. Character is a fundamental measure of a human being

Questions to Ponder:

1. What beliefs that you hold true serve as bedrock for your life?
2. What do you feel should serve as bedrock beliefs and principles for the future of our country?

Part 7

Believing in the Future

Chapter 20
Harsh Reality

To summarize what we have discussed so far... *the interconnected trends of modern technology and seven related forms of societal ammunition loaded into the weapon that is primed to shoot holes in the normalcy, prosperity, and hope of the American Dream are:*

Technology

Identity

Marginalization

Entitlement

Bias

Obsession

Manipulation

Belief

Time bomb definition: *a device with components interconnected and constructed to explode at a specific time. A situation or condition resembling such a bomb portending disastrous consequences in the future.*

Did you miss it, or did you make the connection? Did you see the pattern and recognize that a Time Bomb has been created and is now **Triggered**?

The T-I-M-E-B-O-M-B of this book challenging your thinking has been under construction over the course of the last eight chapters. Did you see it taking shape chapter by chapter? Similarly, the Time Bomb of our society threatening the American Dream has been under construction over the past 20 years. Have you seen it taking shape?

Did you forget to LOOK? Did you fail to heed Ferris Bueller's warning: "Life moves pretty fast. If you don't stop and look around once in a while, you could miss it"?

It's real. Our societal TIME BOMB is wired around key elements of life, including our identity and beliefs. The trigger for the recent arming of the bomb is technology. Today's tech isn't just a tool to understand the world and the universe; it has become a tool to create our own version of reality.

Dr. Sherry Turkle, a professor at the Massachusetts Institute of Technology and founding director of the MIT Initiative on Technology and Self, offers insights in her TED Talk, "Connected but Alone?" She begins by saying, "I'm still excited by technology, but I believe, and I am here to make the case, that we're letting it take us places that we don't want to go."

Dr. Turkle argues that as we expect more from technology, we expect less from each other. She argues that we are not building relationships with each other as much as we are building relationships with technology as if it were a real thing. Dr. Turkle comments on cell phones by saying "... those little devices in our pockets are so psychologically powerful that they not only change what we do, they change who we are." As technology accelerates, we are simultaneously inventing countless ways to redefine ourselves.

That fever is fueled by the ease of commiserating with similarly oppressed online 'victims." Our search for identity gets bogged down in collectivism – the elevation of group and tribe over dignity of the individual. Is it any surprise that two words related to tribe are tribune and tribulation? Tribune can be defined as a group of appointed judges while tribulation means great affliction, distress and suffering.

In our modern world, tribal collectivism is a catalyst for cult-like connection. The internet allows us to define ourselves with greater granularity and to connect with people far outside what our old neighborhoods would have allowed.

The people next door, who were once considered close and trusted friends in previous decades, are now viewed as strangers, yet we easily bond with virtual tribes comprised of people miles away. This real neighbor strangeness gives rise to mistrust, pushing us deeper into gang-like connections of the digital world.

Today, we can have many virtual comrades who fit into our clique or tribe, but sadly, very few genuine relationships. These screen-deep connections are created as quickly as our imaginations allow. Dorothy Gale got it right in the ending scene of *The Wizard of Oz*: when she was awakened from her dream, looking up at family and friends saying "If I ever go looking for my heart's desire again, I won't look any further than my own back yard."

Our search for identity gets bogged down in collectivism – the elevation of group and tribe over dignity of the individual.

A Boisterous Sea of Liberty...
A Struggle for Becoming, Belonging,
   Believing...
Ominous Trends and Troubling Signs...
Wimps, Crybabies and Dummies...
American Dream at Risk...
The Search for Ourselves...
Dissension and Division...
Selfishness Run Amuck...
Discouraging Search for Truth...
Weakness of Mind, Body and Spirit
Attack on Beliefs...

The Harsh Reality

Earlier, we revisited Paul Harvey's 60-year-old radio broadcast, "If I Were the Devil," where he prophesied about emerging societal threats. Today, technology allows us to ask a modern source a similar question – with an eerily similar answer:

Inquiry: *ChatGPT, if you were the devil, how would you destroy the young minds of the next generation without them even knowing it?*

ChatGPT response: *If I were the devil, I wouldn't come with violence, I'd come with convenience. I would give them everything they wanted and strip them of everything they needed. I'd make them feel connected but completely alone, endlessly entertained but quietly empty. I would blur the lines between truth and opinion until nothing meant anything. I'd teach them to chase dopamine not purpose, to worship self but loathe who they are.*

I wouldn't destroy them with war; I'd destroy them with apathy. I'd keep them distracted, numb, and scrolling, always scrolling.

I'd dismantle the family by redefining it, making fathers optional, mothers exhausted, and children confused. I'd hand them a phone before they could speak in complete sentences and I'd would watch their minds rot slowly, sweetly, silently – and the most brilliant part – they'd never know it was me. They'd call it freedom.

Of course, that is not freedom; it is more like 'free-dumb.'

It all started with **Technology,** the accelerant that created a social vacuum. Technology cleverly preyed on an exposed vulnerability, our need for **Identity.** Then that Identity, through the twisted workings of the social media platforms, came under attack by **Marginalization**. To fend off oppression, we sought protection with our shield of **Entitlement.** However, when marginalization was supercharged with **Bias** in a betrayal of truth, we receded too deeply into our own protective cloak of selfish truth, of **Obsession.** Unfortunately, our Obsession made us vulnerable to the power of **Manipulation,** which has torn us apart from our long-held **Beliefs** of who we are and what our purpose in life really is.

The attack on society and freedom levied by the Time Bomb has left us obsessing over our own little worlds, each one teetering out of control. We have become weak. It will take a strong spirit to avoid becoming lifelong victims of this ticking time bomb.

We would be wise to recognize the patterns and avoid the mistakes that plague the wimps, dummies, and crybabies among us. Wimps, often targeted for their identity, are easily browbeat by manipulation. Dummies eternally handcuffed by their limited knowledge and disempowering beliefs, are habitually duped by bias. Crybabies, wrapped in entitlement, are overwhelmed by marginalization. We must learn from them.

The world improves when we become stronger individually and collectively. That begins by recognizing the patterns that brought us here and connecting the dots to find a better way forward.

Chapter 21

Patterns & Framework

Everything is connected. The wiring of the TIME BOMB explains *what* mechanisms are driving the trajectory of society. The explosive elements, ranging from high-powered technology to corrupted beliefs and reckless disregard for common sense, are shaping society into an armed and dangerous incendiary subsistence.

We must now ask, "How about the *why*?" Why is this bomb lurking in our midst? Why are we a hair-trigger away from things blowing up? The answers lie in our believing, belonging, and becoming.

From who we are, to what we believe, to what we do – the story of connection unfolds. By decoding the time bomb, we uncovered core beliefs shaping modern identity. These beliefs are not only connected to our behavior, but they're causal as well.

To see the pattern in our evolving identity, we need a framework—an adaptation of Maslow's hierarchy of needs, refined by Tony Robbins' 6 basic human needs.

These needs, which play to our hearts and souls, build in a natural sequence and dominate at different stages of life:

1. **Certainty**: The need for safety, control, order, and comfort (As a baby who is all consumed with order... to be fed, clean, safe and secure).
2. **Variety**: The need for adventure, change, surprise, and spontaneity (As a toddler or young child who is bent to experiment and endlessly explore in varied play).
3. **Significance**: The need for validation, approval, acceptance, value, and importance (As a teenager striving to prove self-sufficiency and to receive the acceptance of non-parent others).
4. **Connection/Love**: The need for belonging, understanding, closeness, and meaningful relationships (As a young career person looking for professional connection and a love life to boot).
5. **Growth**: An expansion of capacity, capability or understanding (As a middle-aged professional acquiring top skills and moving up the corporate ladder).
6. **Contribution**: A sense of service and focus on helping, giving to and supporting others (As a successful professional who 'has made it' or a retired person looking to give back through philanthropy and/or contributing as a family elder).

Certainty

Certainty comes from knowledge and wisdom – the ability to distinguish what is real from imagined, what is gospel vs. hearsay, what is written in stone vs. fabricated. Early humans evolved as expert pattern-detectors. Over time, the certainty we held in recognizing and responding to these patterns was upgraded by our increasing knowledge and advanced technological tools.

Unfortunately, today, our wisdom is now dumbed down by closed-mindedness, limited debate, and blind certainty. Biased media and nonstop digital noise fuel opinions. Technology accelerates life so fast that certainty is more complicated than ever to grasp.

To cope, many retreat into nostalgia – the comfort of the frozen-in-time "good old days." Gen Z, in particular, is driving a surge of retro cravings; sequels, flashbacks, and vintage styles. Unfortunately, escapism quickly collapses under the weight of reality.

In our current reality, the mentally weak are falling prey to twisted biasing of truth while wimps succumb to the slightest adversity.

Variety

Variety is the spice of life. It makes life interesting. Adventure, novelty, and spontaneity add flavor to exis-tence. Human creativity and technological innovation bring endless variety – but too much of anything becomes overwhelming.

Modern life floods us with choices, creating anxiety,

stress, and decision fatigue. Many cope through instant-gratification fixes that spiral out of control.

Variety's cousin, uncertainty, is cognitively taxing. The *Serenity Prayer* urges wisdom in the face of what we cannot control: "God, grant me the serenity to accept the things I cannot change, the courage to change the things I can and the wisdom to know the difference."At the deepest level it is our beliefs coupled with our values which can bring confidence, hope and faith that our uncertain future will turn out as it should. But wisdom in waning, and so is faith. Many turn to dopamine-driven escapes to numb their fear of the future.

In our current reality, the majority of us, those of limited faith, are spooked about the future while the crybabies among them hold fast to the coping mechanism of instant gratification.

Significance

With a world view that sees our life environment as dark and fearful, we yearn for a silver lining in the dark clouds. We hunger for significance – a sense of worthiness and a need to being seen. Today, garnering attention has become a primary coping mechanism. Social platforms reward validation, creating a vicious cycle of approval-seeking.

Social proof – views, followers, likes – has become a modern measure of value. This obsession breeds narcissism and a needy mentality. People photoshop their image, fabricate personas, and parade online wearing masks. Unfortunately, the self-focus invariably leads to either arrogance or insecurity.

True significance demands authenticity, not attention. Yet many chase virtual relevance, misusing victimhood for sympathy or falling into entitlement as a substitute for purpose. Sage advice is to spend less time pretending and more time becoming.

In our current reality, dummies misappropriate victimhood to relish in virtual significance. Not to be outdone, many wayward souls convert to narcissism and voluntarily take on chronic cases of entitled mentality.

Connection/Love

What we value is what we hold as true, significant and meaningful. Traditionally, family and faith were the centers of love, connection and caring. Regretfully, today, many value virtual friends, influencers, and celebrities more than genuine, in-person relationships.

The lack of genuine relationships creates a deep void. The yearning for caring and intimate connection is grounded in our evolutionary drives to survive, thrive and reproduce. When family and faith decline, people search desperately for something, or someone, to care about.

Case in point: By opting out of marriage and childrearing, many women, are now searching for others to love and care for. Often, they sympathize with and advocate for the downtrodden, the oppressed victims of society. Unfortunately, their care is misdirected maternal instinct that is misspent on imagined victims, who in many cases are miscreants who supposedly have been 'victimized' by the patriarchy, greedy corporations and institutions. Virtue signaling is, for these sympathizers, essentially a dopamine hit disguised as compassion. Look, and you will see how powerful maternal instinct is in the home, when healthy, and how harmful it can be when misdirected.

Tribes on social platforms now serve as substitutes for home. Yet, these groups are often led by ambitious influencers seeking power, not genuine connection. As our world is often framed as a battle between predators and prey, or between the oppressed and the oppressor, we yearn for connection to others who care.

In our current reality, wannabes are thirsting for group identity and marginalizing others while our young adults redefine home in terms of followers not family.

Growth

Growth means gaining knowledge, wisdom, and capability. It is progress, fulfillment, and becoming who we strive to be. However, Machiavellian forces – such as manipulation and coercion – threaten our growth. It is a game of Win-Lose.

Group think, jealousy, envy, pride and other controlling thought patterns and emotions make us vulnerable to a hijacking of our personal liberty. We protect ourselves by nurturing good relationships, holding to our values, and maintaining a growth mindset.

Growth transforms, providing life lessons and a maturity that comes from overcoming adversity. Our identity shifts as life changes – from moving to a new country to marriage, parenthood, and achieving long-term goals. These shifts reflect our growth. Self-actualization – becoming the best version of ourselves – requires purpose, discipline, and grit. Yet many lack commitment, falling into passive lifestyles like Lying Flatism or chronic victimhood. Comfort can indeed be the enemy of growth.

In our current reality, the accomplished and selfish are peddling influence and breeding manipulation while the unprincipled strivers play a false Win-Lose game.

Contribution

Our highest purpose is found outside ourselves – in the positive impact we have on others. Life is about relationships. Without contribution, self-actualization becomes unused potential. Parents, caregivers, leaders, teachers, business owners, and life partners find meaning in lifting others, as we all should.

Epicurean philosophy and Christian virtues both affirm that a meaningful life requires prudence, justice, courage, temperance, faith, hope, and charity. Aristotle taught us courage is the mother of all virtues as it enables all the others.

Faith is foundational. Faith can be considered the quintessential courageous mindset as it abides in an indomitable spirit of peace and pure love. This spirit, is an enabler of the most potent confidence that rises when you allow the power of God to go before you.

Actual contribution is selfless. Fake contribution is a form of virtue signaling, where self-promotion is disguised as service.

A meaningful life flows from strong, virtuous beliefs and from creating a life of value using our gifts to uplift others. As we are created in His image we are co-creators with God.

In our current reality, limited belief change agents squander their positive impact while we witness virtue signalers masquerading as Superheroes.

A 6 Needs Summary...

Through our knowledge of the world, we gain certainty about the patterns of things, like the chorus of a familiar song. But certainty breeds familiarity and predictability, which can become the monotonous same ol', same ol' refrain. So, we seek variety and spontaneity as in a jazz jam session, which, if unchecked, can breed a dependence on immediate gratification —a dopamine rush in the moment.

Over the long term though, it is experiences, both upbeat and sobering, that shape us as we embark on a journey of becoming our true and significant selves. Following significance, it is harmony of connection that we yearn for as we search for identity in the community and accompaniment of others. Far too often many fall short of their potential, singing off-key or dancing off rhythm never realizing the personal growth necessary to make a real difference in the world.

For the few purpose-driven difference makers, those who spurn the ways of wimps, dummies, and crybabies, life can become a meaningful journey paired to a symphony of purpose.

	6 HUMAN NEEDS	Ugly Manifestations and Failures
BELIEVING	Certainty	The Mentally Weak Falling Prey to Twisted Biasing of Truth
	Comfort, Safety, Security	Wimps Succumbing to the Slightest Adversity
	Variety	Those of Limited Faith Fearing a Spooky Future
	Uncertainty, Surprise	Crybabies Craving for Instant Gratification
BELONGING	Significance	Dummies Misappropriating Victimhood to Gain Attention
	Importance, Worth, Value	Narcissists Obsessing with an Entitled Mentality
	Connection	Wannabes Thirsting for Group Identity; Marginalizing Others
	Love, Empathy, Care	Young Adults Redefining Home as Followers not Family
BECOMING	Growth	The Elite Peddling Influence & Breeding Manipulation
	Achieve, Attain, Wisdom	Unprincipled Strivers Playing a false Game of Win-Lose
	Contribution	Limited Belief Change Agents Squandering Positive Impact
	Giving, Generosity, Legacy	Virtue Signallers Masquerading as Super Heroes

5 Roadblocks on our path to fulfillment:

1. Traditional institutional identities and beliefs, including family and faith, are under attack
2. We are becoming wimps, crybabies, and dummies
3. We increasingly identify only with our group
4. Victim mentality is rampaging; Oppression is a new cultural sport
5. As a country and people, we are DIVIDED.

Chapter 22
The Depth of our Division

We are divided. Perhaps as deeply as during the Civil War of the 1860s. As Abraham Lincoln said in his speech to close the Illinois Republican State Convention in 1858 "A house divided against itself cannot stand."

Can the current state of affairs keep our house standing? Could we be approaching the calamity of another civil war? Are we on the verge of fracturing into tribal factions divided by state lines or the urban-rural dichotomy? The divisiveness tearing at our democratic republic has been sensationalized in modern media. Two recent films illustrate this growing unease:

Leave the World Behind (2023). An apocalyptic thriller about a nationwide panic that erupts following cyberattacks and power blackouts, where social order collapses and chaos reigns.

Civil War (2024). Another apocalyptic thriller that follows journalists traveling through a war-torn America, from New York City to Washington, D.C., caught between authoritarian forces and secessionist states like California and Texas.

Both entertaining films dramatize the same question: could division and distrust grow into outright conflict? No doubt these films garnered a good deal of attention as they played on a common sentiment that America's national unity is slipping.

Might we be on the verge of living through a civil war in the next chapter of American history? Will the extremists in our midst be successful in fueling an insurgency that could break our nation apart?

Civil War: Symptoms of Inevitability

1. **Political Polarization:** Politicians are stirring up dissension rather than fostering unity, focusing on opponents' failures rather than seeking solutions.
2. **Tribal Socialization:** We are becoming increasingly tribal in our socialization, clustering into separate enclaves on social networks that reinforce partisan views.
3. **Echoes of History:** "Today's events bear an uncanny resemblance to the 1850's" wrote one author in *Politico*. "Everyone is mad about something, and everyone has a gun."
4. **Public Fear:** A 2022 Rasmussen survey found 50% of respondents believed a civil war could happen "in the next few years."

5. **Demographic Anxiety:** Many fear that immigration is reshaping America's cultural and political landscape, fueling a populist backlash.
6. **Separatist Movements:**
    - Greater Idaho Movement – Eastern Oregon counties seeking to join Idaho
    - Calexit – A California independence campaign
    - Texan Nationalist Movement – advocating for state sovereignty
    - NHEXIT – New Hampshire's bid for independence

Civil War: Factors Moderating the Threat

1. **Scale and Diversity:** Civil wars require mass mobilization around one issue; America's size, diversity, and economic interdependence make that unlikely.
2. **Military Strength:** The U.S. military has 1.3 million active-duty personnel capable of quickly and precisely eliminating threats.
3. **Law Enforcement Cohesion:** From local police to Homeland Security, our institutions remain unified and capable of suppressing insurrection.
4. **Lack of Incentive:** A civil war would devastate corporate, political, and military interests – none of which would gain from the chaos.

5. **Mobility and Integration:** Unlike the 1800s, Americans move freely across states for work and lifestyle, blending regions and reducing isolation.
6. **Connectedness:** Technology and communication – ironically, the sources of division – also bind us together. We can text, call, and video chat across the country in seconds. This connectedness is a stabilizing force.

Are we Headed to Civil War?

Will our country continue to fracture further, decomposing into civil war? Or, will cooler heads prevail and extinguish the fanning flames of division?

What truth will play out?

More importantly, which role will you play?

Chapter 23
Connecting the Dots

Within the 6 Human Needs framework, we find a common link among *Believing*, *Belonging*, and *Becoming*. Phrases such as twisted biasing of truth, future with limited faith, breeding manipulation, misappropriating victimhood, redefining home, and masquerading as superheroes, all point to one central theme – Truth.

Truth and faith are interrelated, as our truth is shaped by belief. Our beliefs about the future show up as hope – or, at their strongest, as faith. Our relentless search for truth defines our humanity. Yet bias and emotion often derail that pursuit. Finding and living by truth and walking in faith are challenges paramount to our fulfillment.

When it comes to truth, though, there is THE Truth, SOCIAL Truth, and finally, YOUR Truth.

It starts and ends with THE truth. THE truth emerges from our need for *Certainty* and *Variety* – fact-based believing. It comes from observing how the world works, understanding cause and effect, and recognizing proven reality. Honest facts, tested ideas, and accurate accounts are the linchpin of THE Truth.

SOCIAL Truth arises from our needs for *Significance* and *Connection*. It shapes how we belong – how we communicate, interact, and build relationships. True social wisdom lies in knowing when to adopt, challenge, or contribute to SOCIAL Truth with integrity and discernment.

YOUR Truth is born of *Growth* and *Contribution*. It's how we become who we're meant to be – developing skills and pursuing purpose and impact. It guides not only the individual but also the collective, where communities align around shared understanding and purpose.

Your identity, a form of belief, is the glue that holds your unique life story together. That story can be a successful and purposeful one only when YOUR Truth aligns with THE Truth.

Sadly, if your truth strays, if you give more credence to your feelings rather than to the truth, which is unfortunately quite common today, then your truth can be a debilitating force holding you back from your potential.

Jeff Bezos, founder of Amazon, in his conversation with Thomas Chua's Steady Compounding podcast, reflects on this tension:

"We humans are not really truth-seeking animals. We are social animals. And take you back in time 10,000 years, and you're in a small village. If you go along to get along, you can survive and procreate. If you're the village truth teller, you might get clubbed to death in the middle of the night. Truths are often, they don't want to be heard because important truths can be uncomfortable, they can be awkward, they can be exhausting. Bezos adds "Any high performing organization has to have mechanisms and a culture that supports truth telling."

Bezo's insight captures how social pressures often overpower honesty, how SOCIAL Truth can be used to circumvent THE Truth. Indeed, truth competes with bias, influence, and convenience. THE Truth is grounded in common sense, science, and Technology yet even these can be obscured by Manipulation or subordinated to strong Beliefs.

SOCIAL Truth, or untruth, often arises from society twisting the interpersonal elements of the TIME BOMB: Marginalization, Bias, and Manipulation.

YOUR Truth is shaped by Identity, Entitlement, Obsession, and Beliefs.

A word of caution: don't be deceived by "truths" rooted in selfishness, coercion, or weakness of character – they collapse under time and scrutiny. Reality and timeless, objective truth always win out.

Unfortunately, it is all too common for folks to subjugate objective truth to a self-serving narrative. As we aim for the highest Maslow needs level of Self-Actualization, the fake, the self-absorbed, the untethered, and the confused among us struggle through the levels immediately below: Belonging and Self-Esteem. The needs hierarchy indeed is significantly self-centered.

Maslow recognized this and, years after introducing his hierarchy of needs, added a topmost level of human consciousness, the peak of human experience known as Self-Transcendence.

Self-transcendence can be defined as follows: Being Self-transcendent is to transcend (or elevate) oneself above self-orientation to that which is greater than the self. It is the realization that individuals are part of a greater whole, a certain oneness, which encompasses humankind in general, the universe, or divine power.

Transcendence is commonly sought through helping others, connecting with nature, and engaging in spiritual practices. In the process of transcending, one comes upon a deeper appreciation of THE Truth, in harmony with the truth of God, of the universe, and of one's own beliefs and destiny.

Chapter 24

Decision-Making Crossroad

Are we running out of time in our search for a truth that can shape a prosperous future? Not yet, but the time bomb is triggered and ticking, and its fuse is short. Can truth, transcendence, and unity be sufficient to lift us above division and help us reclaim the pioneering spirit of our Founding Fathers – the spirit that made the American Dream real and envied across the world? Perhaps yes.

It's time to defuse the time bomb and make things right. It's time to slow down our fast-paced world and take a close look at the trends shaping our world. We need to identify and neutralize the threats to our way of life.

Thomas Paine warned that people often defend what's wrong out of habit, mistaking comfort for truth. The beliefs embedded in our modern TIME BOMB must be dismantled with reason and courage. Resistance to change is inevitable, but common sense and conviction must prevail. To rebuild our world, we must learn from the past, understand the present, and act decisively for the future. Past, present and future are all connected and ultimately fashioned consistent with an evolving truth.

Strong convictions do not necessarily signal a powerful sense of self: Very often quite the opposite. Intensely held beliefs may be no more than a person's unconscious effort to build a sense of Self to fill what, underneath, is experienced as a vacuum.

— *Dr. Gabor Maté*

Charles Dickens illustrated this beautifully in *A Christmas Carol,* where Scrooge was provoked into taking stock of his lot in life. As he did, he experienced a rebirth as he sought to find the truth about his past, present, and future. His rebirth was provoked by the insights provided to him by three spirits or ghosts. With their help, he recognized how his past decisions had consistently eroded his compassion for others and pushed him to be more self-centered. He saw the reality of his present in terms of important things that he had wrongly avoided. And he visualized his likely future if he continued in his present ways.

In the story, after a rebirth of sorts, Scrooge wakes up and realizes he is not a prisoner of his limited beliefs.

He fully understood that he could choose to change. And through that truth, he came to grace in a spiritual awakening.

It takes a willingness for self-reflection, discernment and a threshold level of commitment to see things clearly for what they truly are before we can make the choice to change. The truth shall set you free and it did so for Scrooge.

Like Scrooge, we all possess a superpower: the Power of Choice.

You choose the skills to develop, the battles to fight, and the relationships to nurture. You also choose among various opportunities to take advantage of or let slip by. You choose or decide what doors to open and which doors to close during your limited lifetime on this planet.

Ultimately, you are the captain of your destiny, the architect of your adventure, and the master of your fate. Many drift through life without direction – but even drifting is still a choice. The most powerful choice is choosing to become the shepherd of your soul and the hero of your journey as there's no better way to go through life.

The cup of *having* is never full enough, but the cup of *becoming* fills endlessly with the essence of who you truly are.

Imagine you are holding a cup of coffee when someone bumps into your arm, causing it to spill everywhere.

The question isn't so much who bumped you or why, but why was *coffee* spilled. Why was coffee in your cup and not tea or something else? The point is this: life will shake you up, and whatever is inside of you will spill out. Everyone can only fake what's inside of them for so long; sooner or later, life will poke at you, and you'll show what's inside.

The question then, should be – What fills me?

Is it joy, gratitude, peace, and humility, or is it anger, bitterness, a victim's mentality, and desperation?

Life provides the cup; YOU choose how to fill it.

To become our best selves, each of us must exercise our superpower of choice to fill our cup with purpose. We are the sum of our decisions. Over time, those choices define us—and collectively shape our nation. Real change requires patience and discipline, a steady tide, not a sudden storm.

This   - OR-   That

Claiming **Entitlement**	Accepting **Responsibility**
Being Disingenuous & **Fake**	Being Real and **Authentic**
Being a Consummate **Coward**	Being a **Courageous Contributor**
Identifying by Gender/Skin	Finding **Identity in Purpose**
Playing the **Victim** /Wimp	Making a **Positive Difference**
Being a Chronic **Crybaby**	Being Eternally **Grateful**
Virtue Signaling	Living **Virtuously**
Being an **Activist**	Being a Person of **Positive Action**
Conspiring **Division**	Inspiring **Common Vision**
Overindulging Today	Preparing a **Successful Future**
Being Fat, **Dumb** and Happy	Seeking Knowledge & **Wisdom**
Being **Burdened by the Dark**	Being **Emboldened by the Light**

It's Your Choice!   It's Your Life.   It's our World.

Here's the bad news: Time Flies.

Here's the good news: You're the pilot.

Spend less time pretending, more time becoming.

. . .

This country is nearing a crossroads – an inflection point in our nation's journey. To move forward, we must reclaim the spirit that built this country and raised the sail of the American Dream on the boisterous sea of liberty.

Our success will demand faith, purpose, and perseverance. For us to overcome and for our country to thrive, will require an unwavering belief in a prosperous tomorrow. It will require a new beginning- a turning point of sorts.

It will require a rediscovery of our National Identity. In the spirit of that oft-seen phrase on the back of our one-dollar bill: Novus Ordo Seclorum. Novus ordo seclorum is a Latin phrase that translates to "a New Order of the Ages." It will take discipline, grit, and social responsibility to resist self-indulgence and to embrace virtue.

Ultimately, to defuse the bomb, it will take conquering the forces of distrust, winning a victory over disbelief, and quelling dissension on the battleground of truth. It will take a return to common sense and a united effort with cohesion of purpose and the fire of ambition to stay the course.

Jim Rohn, American entrepreneur, author, and mentor to the successful, famously said, "We must suffer from one of two pains: the pain of discipline or the pain of regret. Discipline weighs ounces while regret weighs tons."

Confronted with Rohn's challenge, it is heartening to

know that folks who persevere with grit and determination often emerge on the other side with renewed purpose.

The choice for you is yours:

- Suppress your true self to gain the acceptance of strangers or live authentically.
- Depend entirely on others for the sake of making it in this world or take responsibility and be self-sufficient.
- *Abandon* belief in God and country or stand firm even when it costs you.

Our success will demand faith, purpose, and perseverance. For us to overcome and for our country to thrive, will require an unwavering belief in a prosperous tomorrow. It will require a new beginning – a turning point of sorts.

It's time to trigger the best in you. Don't die with the music still in you. Find your God-given talent. Find your talent, your gift, and play it for all to hear!

What will you Believe?
Where will you Belong?
Who will you Become?

The opposite of courage is not cowardice, it is conformity. Even a dead fish can go with the flow.

— Jim Hightower

We must join forces, individually and collectively to diffuse this potentially world-changing time bomb. We, who want to keep our country on the same path it has been on since its inception, need to make the right choices and embrace our shared vision. That vision, captured in the motto E pluribus unum (out of many one), must inspire us to reclaim our united identity despite any differences we have. While diversity is our foundation, it is unity that is our enduring strength.

If you are a believer in the ideals expressed in this book, you are in the majority. However, the opposition – wimps and crybabies- drown us out. Not because they yell louder, it's because too many in the majority are silent! We believers see what's going on, but fear backlash from a vocal, wild-and-woolly minority.

The silent majority has a duty to rise, to devote a passionate adherence to principle, family, and faith to overcome distrust, disbelief, and division.

We need to embody the initiative Mahatma Gandhi spoke of, "You must be the change you wish to see in the world."

Let us not forget the spirit of our Founding Fathers who formulated the greatest experiment in democracy.

That "experiment" must live on, and it will, through courage, faith, common sense – and us uniting with purpose and strength of belief. To succeed, we must have faith in America.

Undoubtedly the work ahead will require effort and personal responsibility. It will require a united effort with cohesion of purpose and the fire of ambition to stay the course. It will require the ability to sacrifice and the fortitude to overcome the addiction to instant gratification. It is all worthy of our dedication.

Our victorious fight will be like winning the battle over the enticement of the marshmallow and earning two later. Or the alternative, a detonation of the bomb wreaking havoc and widespread destruction because we succumbed to increasing decadence and let the marshmallows win...

S'mores anyone?

My name is Patrick Leask, and I want to thank you for reading this book.

I would be honored to deliver a keynote, moderate a panel, or participate in a panel discussion, speak on your podcast, radio show, or TV show, and engage in corporate and community town halls, respectfully articulating the significant challenges this great country faces from within.

I have customizable Signature Talks:

1. *Removing the Mask:* Making authenticity your ticket to personal freedom.
2. *Path to Wisdom:* Practical ways to bridge the gap between thinking and knowing.
3. *Becoming:* The six human needs and a path from significance to contribution.
4. *Believing:* The counterintuitive harmony between science and religion
5. *Belonging:* The risk and reward of social bonding

Booking + Press:
Email: ________________________________
Phone/Text: (###) ###-####
Website: ________________________________

Lastly, I want to say, God Bless You, and God Bless the United States of America.

Afterword

As suggested in an earlier chapter of this book, "It is now a good time for a little introspection into the best that lies within us and whether that potential is threatened, thwarted, or just waiting to be ignited."

Introspection shows that the threat to American prosperity is real. The American Dream is in peril. Social and political polarization feels more divisive than ever, economic uncertainty weighs on working families, and the digital world often leaves us more isolated than connected. Yet despite these troubling winds, the enduring sparks and smoldering embers of the American spirit appear to be rekindling a fire of ambition and hope. Over the past couple of years, there have been a few signs of a purposeful becoming beginning to flare.

The American Dream

The Archbridge Institute, from their "American Dream 2025 Snapshot" June 2025, laid it out simply. There is some good news and there is some bad news. While nearly 6 in 10 respondents in their study cited poor economic conditions as their biggest obstacle, only 30% said the American Dream is out of reach. The economic headwinds cited included rising housing prices, high cost of living, and low wages among other financial factors. Despite these challenges, Archbridge, reports that 7 in 10 Americans are indeed optimistic about the American Dream. Fewer people believe the American Dream is out of reach than in 2024.

Within neighborhoods, workplaces, and families, Americans are beginning to reminisce about times past, reflecting on the timeless values of the American Dream. Values that built this land of opportunity from self-determination and a pioneering spirit to the belief that freedom and responsibility go hand in hand. There are other signs too. Signs of renewed interest in community, family, and faith.

Work Ethic, Responsibility & Opportunity

Entrepreneurship

One of the most evident signs of this renewal of the American spirit is the surge in entrepreneurship. In 2023 alone, according to the U.S. Census Bureau, Americans filed a record 5.5 million new business applications. Many of these startups are microbusinesses or family-run ventures, suggesting a shift toward self-determination and community-level economic empowerment rather than the stable but bureaucratic work environment of corporate life.

This surge in small business creation reflects a desire to take risks, build livelihoods, and create opportunities for others. This is the heart of the American Dream: the conviction that with effort, imagination, and persistence, one can shape one's own destiny.

<u>Financial Responsibility</u>

In addition, it looks like young adults, specifically those representing Gen Z (age 13 to 25), are pushing a trend toward their own financial responsibility. A study published July 30, 2025 from Bank of America's 2025 Better Money Habits® makes this case. The study found that Gen Z feels a lack of income is a problem, with over half (53%) not feeling they make enough money to live the life they want, and many are struggling to save consistently. Despite these sentiments, many young adults are tackling their financial challenges with discipline.

Key findings from the Gen Z money management study include:

- Over the past year, 72% of Gen Zers took steps to improve their financial health, such as

putting money toward savings (51%) or paying down debt (24%).
- Nearly two-thirds (64%) of the cohort focused on reducing expenses – 41% cut back on dining out, and 23% shopped at more affordable grocery stores.

The study also found that more young adults are taking full responsibility for their own finances. While 39% receive financial support from parents and other family members, this is down from 46% a year ago.

<u>Responsible Behavior</u>

Beyond finances, our younger generations are exhibiting more responsible behavior when it comes to smoking, drinking, and drugs. As of late, through September 2025, the overarching trend is that overall teen alcohol and illicit drug use is at historically low levels and continues to decline from pre-pandemic rates.

According to recent data from the National Survey on Drug Use and Health (NSDUH) and Monitoring the Future (MTF) survey for 2024, rates of substance use among teens have hit some of the lowest levels in decades. For example:

- Only 25.8% of 12th graders reported using marijuana in the past year, the lowest level in three decades.
- Annual alcohol consumption among 12th graders dropped to 41.7% in 2024 (down from

45.7% in 2023 and a remarkable 75% in 1997).

- Cigarette use among 12- to 20-year-olds remained low, at 3.3%.
- Prescription narcotic abuse among high school seniors reached an all-time low: only 0.6% in 2024, compared to 9.5% in 2004.

Opportunity through Education

Our institutions, too, are beginning to break from past self-serving motives to a responsible pursuit of the well-being of our youngest citizens. This commitment can be found in the pioneering of new age methods of K through 12 education that are opening new doors of opportunity for our kids.

One example of innovation in education can be found at Alpha School which has expanded rapidly from the original campus in Austin, TX to schools in San Francisco, Miami, Los Angeles, Washington DC, Dallas, and other metro areas.

At Alpha School, students complete all their academic work in just two hours. They spend 30 minutes a day on each of four core subjects — math, reading, language, and science. Oh, and there are no teachers, either. Instead, artificial intelligence leads the way. That's right. Alpha School leverages the latest technology to provide an exceptional educational experience.

Kids learn at their own pace, with one-on-one instruction from AI tutors. And the students are thriving — outperforming their peers in traditional schools by leaps and bounds. This new age education model gives children extra hours each day to engage in workshops and creative projects, pursuing their true passions.

Schools like Alpha School represent a significant shift to a new microschool model that emphasizes flexibility, personalized learning, and the integration of technology to create new opportunities for learning and personal growth.

Community, Family Life & Faith

<u>Community</u>

Socializing in real life (IRL) is becoming a thing again in 2025. Driven by a post-pandemic desire for both authentic communion and a reprieve from constant screen exposure, folks are seeking more real human connection.

- Increased Demand for In-Person Events: Event organizers are planning more in-person experiences, with 66% anticipating an increase in such events in 2025. Conferences, workshops, and social events are in vogue.
- Rise of Social Clubs and Activity-Based Socializing: There's a growing trend of people joining specific clubs and groups based on shared interests (e.g., running clubs, book clubs, pickleball leagues) to meet people in a structured, low-pressure environment.

- A Focus on Wellness and Meaningful Experiences: Consumers are prioritizing mental well-being and seeking "experiential living" through activities like wellness retreats, group fitness sessions, and unique, one-time gatherings.

The uptick in IRL socialization reflects a broader cultural shift towards valuing deep relationships and experiences over materialism and virtual connections.

<u>Family Life</u>

Valuing family life remains a high priority for most people. Recent data from 2025 shows that it is, in some contexts, becoming even more central to people's lives.

Key trends in 2025 related to valuing family life include:

- Top Stated Value: A June 2025 Gallup-Aspen Ideas survey found that 49% of Americans say family is their single most important value, ranking significantly higher than any other value, such as freedom (30%).
- Multigenerational Living on the Rise: Driven by economic pressures, rising housing costs, and the desire for mutual support (e.g., childcare and eldercare), more families are choosing to live in multigenerational households. This trend fosters closer bonds across generations.

- Workplace Flexibility for our parents: Flexible work arrangements (remote/hybrid) and supportive workplace policies (paid parental leave, on-site childcare) are becoming crucial for modern parents seeking better work-life harmony.
- Modernizing Family Values: While the importance of family remains strong, the definition of family is evolving. Parenting trends in 2025 show embrace and support for extended families, blended households, and co-parenting setups.

Overall, while family structures are evolving and diversifying, the fundamental importance of family life is widely affirmed and is a significant force shaping lifestyle choices and societal trends in 2025.

<u>Faith</u>

After years of decline, a growing number of Americans believe religion is on its way back, a new study from Pew Research Center suggests. In their October 2025 report on religion, Pew found that Americans' views about religion in public life are shifting. In their February 2025 survey, 31% of U.S. adults said religion was gaining influence in American life – the highest figure seen in 15 years.Other indicators of faith resurgence in America:

- Bible sales were up 22% in 2024 and 36% in

the month of September 2025 versus September 2024.

- Church attendance is up, with young adults showing the largest increase.
- Spiritual and religious revival is making a comeback.

There are numerous examples of religious revivals across America. Turning Point USA continues to gain influence and momentum after Charlie Kirk's death. Turning Point USA, which expanded its Christian-based influence to dozens of new college campuses in 2025, is sparking a religious stir among young adults. Another example is the extended prayer session that took place at Asbury University in Wilmore, Kentucky.

The Asbury Revival began in February 2023 during a regular chapel service and lasted 16 days. The news of the phenomenon quickly spread through social media and in Christian online publications. The Christian revival was a nonstop, two-week prayer session culminating in a final student service on February 23rd. The event grew from a few dozen students to tens of thousands of visitors from around the world, attracting significant media attention before university officials officially ended the on-campus gatherings.

The prayer sessions were attended by approximately 15,000 people each day. By its end, the Asbury Revival brought 50,000–70,000 visitors to Wilmore, representing more than 200 academic institutions and multiple countries. "It is a story that we are all still learning, and it is a story that is still being written," said Asbury faculty member Jeannie Banter.

Exceptionalism and Common Sense

The fire to be ignited, to fulfill the promise of America, has exceptionalism as fuel. The term 'American Exceptionalism' was coined by French political scientist and historian Alexis de Tocqueville. Following his travels here in 1831, de Tocqueville expressed a belief that the United States is distinctive and exemplary compared to other nations. He is quoted as saying, "The greatness of America lies not in being more enlightened than any other nation, but rather in her ability to repair her faults".

American exceptionalism endures not as mythology, but as a lived culture rooted in the elements of the American Dream:

- Faith in individual agency
- Pride in honest work
- A moral drive toward contribution and community
- Resilience through adversity
- A deep-seated optimism about the future.

Even in the face of division, most Americans share more values than the headlines we see every day suggest. Studies from More in Common reveal that two-thirds of Americans still agree on foundational principles —fairness, freedom, and opportunity for all.

The so-called "exhausted majority" is rejecting

extremism and quietly choosing unity over outrage. They may not dominate the news cycle, but they embody the steady, common sense, and pragmatic optimism that has long characterized the American people.

So, while the challenges of our time are real, they are not signs of decline. They are catalysts for rediscovery that honor the past while embracing the future. Americans are remembering what has always made this country unique: a belief in individual effort combined with a commitment to the common good; faith in the future tempered by responsibility in the present; and an unshakable conviction that no matter how divided we seem, our shared ideals are stronger than what separates us.

America's story has always been one of challenge met by courage and hardship overcome by heart. Once again, the people of this nation are showing that even in divided times, the spirit still burns and the dream lives on. Faith, family, and freedom remain its compass; perseverance and hope, its path forward. The quiet renewal has begun, and with it, the enduring promise of the American Dream.

About the Author

Patrick is a truth tinkerer, a soul explorer, and an insight engineer. Throughout his 30-year career, Patrick applied his engineering training to problem-solving in large-scale construction project management. In a shift from process to people, he transitioned into marketing, where he helped operations managers see the true value of custom solutions. Later, Patrick led a business team to create new methods and products before moving from his corporate role to becoming an entrepreneur as a coach and consultant.

As a coach to many, Patrick uses his keen insight and analytical ability to create a big-picture view from a myriad of details and perspectives. He regularly hosts seminars and workshops on a variety of topics, including personal productivity, marketing strategy, selling techniques, business growth & profitability, leadership, and team building.

Being a lifelong learner and father, Patrick has a passion for passing on his knowledge and wisdom. In addition to coaching, he creates content for online learning systems tailored to entrepreneurs who are looking for a system, a knowledge base, and the right tools to grow their business.

Patrick is a passionate creator of games, from personalized, fun workshop exercises to invented leisure time activities and several original games for family get-togethers.

Patrick is Dad to two children, a brother to a brother and sister, a relative of a loving extended family, a proud descendant of Scottish heritage, a patriotic American, and an active member in an inspiring church community.

Recommended Reading

1. *The Constitution of Knowledge: A Defense of Truth* by Jonathan Rauch

Jonathan Rauch argues that truth in free societies emerges from a fragile "constitution of knowledge": shared norms of evidence and open debate. He shows how disinformation and tribalism threaten this system and offers principles for defending a common, reality-based public life.

2. *Alone Together: Why we Expect More from Technology and Less From Each Other* by Sherry Turkle

Sherry Turkle explores how social media and tech tools promise connection yet leave us emotionally isolated. Drawing on interviews and research, she shows how constant digital contact can erode empathy and weaken relationships.

3. *12 Rules for Life* by Jordan Peterson

Jordan Peterson's 12 Rules for Life blends psychology, myth, and practical advice to argue that meaning comes from responsibility, discipline, and truth-telling. He urges readers to speak honestly, confront chaos, and orient their lives toward purpose rather than comfort or resentment.

4. *Digital Liturgies: Rediscovering Christian Wisdom in an Online Age* by Samuel D. James

Samuel D. James argues that the internet is not a neutral tool but an environment that quietly shapes our loves, beliefs, and habits. He contrasts "digital liturgies," with historic Christian wisdom offering practical guidance for meaning and purpose living faithfully before Christ.